A STORY OF UKRAINIAN FORCED LABOUR,
THE LEICA CAMERA FACTORY,
AND NAZI RESISTANCE

THE

MATRYOSHKA
MEMOIRS

SASHA COLBY

Published by ECW Press
665 Gerrard Street East
Toronto, Ontario, Canada m4m 1y2
416-694-3348 / info@ecwpress.com

Editor for the Press: Susan Renouf
Copy editor: Jen Albert
Cover design: Jessica Albert
Front cover photography: (Right, Elsie Kühn-Leitz) © Ernst Leitz Foundation, courtesy of Oliver Nass. (Left, Irina Kylynych Nikifortchuk) courtesy of Alex Nikifortchuk.

To the best of her abilities, the author has related experiences, places, people, and organizations from his memories of them. In order to protect the privacy of others, she has, in some instances, changed the names of certain people and details of events and places.

LIBRARY AND ARCHIVES CANADA CATALOGUING IN PUBLICATION

Title: The Matryoshka memoirs : a story of Ukrainian forced labour, the Leica camera factory, and Nazi resistance / Sasha Colby.

Names: Colby, Sasha, 1978- author.

Identifiers: Canadiana (print) 20230237150 | Canadiana (ebook) 20230237185

ISBN 978-1-77041-735-9 (softcover)
ISBN 978-1-77852-214-7 (Kindle)
ISBN 978-1-77852-213-0 (PDF)
ISBN 978-1-77852-212-3 (ePub)

Subjects: LCSH: Nikifortchuk, Irina. | LCSH: Kühn-Leitz, Elsie, 1903-1985. | LCSH: Foreign workers, Ukrainian—Germany—Biography. | LCSH: World War, 1939-1945—Women—Germany—Biography. | LCSH: Ukrainians—Germany—Biography. | LCSH: Women—Germany—Biography. | LCSH: World War, 1939-1945—Conscript labor—Germany. | LCGFT: Biographies.

Classification: LCC D805.G3 C65 2023 | DDC 940.54/05—dc23

This book is funded in part by the Government of Canada. *Ce livre est financé en partie par le gouvernement du Canada.* We acknowledge the support of the Canada Council for the Arts. *Nous remercions le Conseil des arts du Canada de son soutien.* We acknowledge the funding support of the Ontario Arts Council (OAC), an agency of the Government of Ontario. We also acknowledge the support of the Government of Ontario through the Ontario Book Publishing Tax Credit, and through Ontario Creates.

PRINTED AND BOUND IN CANADA   PRINTING: FRIESENS   5   4   3   2   1

MIX
Paper from responsible sources
FSC® C016245

"In *The Matryoshka Memoirs*, Sasha Colby draws together treasures from oral history, meticulous research, and her own imagination to tell 'A Story of Ukrainian Forced Labour, the Leica Camera Factory, and Nazi Resistance,' but also of three, and eventually four, generations of women whose conversations and memories range from Eastern to Western Europe, from Eastern to Western Canada, and from past horrors to the intense, loving family dynamics of recent days. The writing is vivid and lyrical, the narratives are arresting, and the women are unforgettable."

— CRAIG HOWES, Director, Center for Biographical Research, University of Hawai'i at Mānoa

"From the moment I began reading *The Matryoshka Memoirs*, I was transported. Colby's memoir moves seamlessly between time and place, fact, fiction, and memory bringing us along with her as we travel from safety one moment, to terrifying circumstances the next. Evocative, poetic and at times stark and direct, Colby invites us into the intimate circle of her family, where she weaves the ordinary and the unimaginable together to create a deeply affecting work that explores a hidden history and the depth of feeling within. Through this beautifully written memoir, we are able to touch and feel the experience of one woman, one family and the countless others who have stories such as these still waiting to be told."

— DOROTHY DITTRICH, 2022 Governor General's Award winner for drama

"Colby skillfully weaves together the stories of women brought together by war and its remembering and forgetting. This is both a captivating family memoir of a granddaughter coaxing stories from her grandmother and Colby's recreation of the wartime meeting of a Ukrainian forced labourer and a wealthy German woman. I picked it up and couldn't put it down."

— TIM COLE, University of Bristol, Director of the Brigstow Institute, author of *Holocaust Landscapes*

"This exquisitely wrought book paints a compelling picture of one woman's journey through the labour camps of Europe in the 1940s. Woven into her story are the stories of the women of her family, from her daughter to great-granddaughter. This is a delicate, poignant, and deeply humane exploration of generational inheritance, legacy, and female survival."

— KATE KENNEDY, BBC broadcaster and Associate Director, Oxford Centre for Life-writing, University of Oxford

*For my
grandmother,
mother,
and daughter*

*Christmas 1956 — My grandmother Irina,
grandfather Sergei, and mother, Lucy, age six*

AUTHOR'S NOTE

AT LEAST TWELVE MILLION PEOPLE WERE brought to Germany as forced labourers during World War II. Approximately three-quarters were civilian deportees, the rest prisoners of war. At its height, foreign forced labour accounted for roughly twenty percent of Germany's wartime workforce, the majority from Nazi-conquered territories in Central and Eastern Europe.

In *Hitler's Foreign Workers*, Ulrich Herbert notes that in 1944, "more than half of the Polish and Soviet civilian workers were female, their average age around twenty." Replacement labour for German men fighting the war, foreign forced labourers were distributed among Germany's farms, mines, and factories.

One of these factories, Ernst Leitz Optical Industry, known as Leitz Werke, belonged to the prominent Leitz family. The factory made optical equipment and Leica cameras crucial to Nazi military and propaganda efforts. Ernst Leitz II and his daughter, Elsie Kühn-Leitz, opposed the Nazi regime. However, under threat of detainment and company expropriation, Ernst Leitz II supplied the German military and staffed the factory with foreign forced labour; the camp was policed by the Gestapo. Elsie Kühn-Leitz, who had formerly worked in the Leitz company's accounting office, made herself responsible for overseeing the welfare of the factory's female "Eastern workers." My maternal grandmother, Irina Kylynych Nikifortchuk, was one of them. This story is a combination of oral history, research, and imagination. Much of the historical dialogue has been fictionalized. Some chronologies have been condensed. Minor characters my grandmother remembered faintly have been fleshed out and named; where not enough information was available, others have been omitted. Elsie Kühn-Leitz's essay about the events of 1943 has been divided into sections, interwoven with details drawn from other first-person accounts of forced labour camps and women's prisons, and dramatized.

June 1942

SUMMER LIGHT SLIPS THROUGH THE SLATS of the livestock car. Irina presses her cheek against the rough wood, seeking a cool breath of air beyond the heat and press of bodies. When the train stops, new prisoners are crowded in. All of them are young. Each day the German soldiers give the prisoners one piece of dark bread and one cup of water. There are no latrines, only straw, and as the crowding intensifies so does the stench. It is a smell that nauseates the prisoners and causes the guards to look more remote by the day.

June 1942
Wetzlar, Germany

ELSIE PLACES THE COVER OVER HER typewriter and returns the files to the metal cabinet beside her desk. Her movements are clipped, a way of managing tension over events now out of her control: the ability of two little girls to stay quiet, their mother's nerve at the border, the skill and discretion of the forger. When Maria appears in the doorway, Elsie tries not to startle. She locks the cabinet, drops the key into her jacket pocket, smooths her dark-blonde hair with the flat of her hand. Maria's large blue eyes are full of questions, which Elsie deflects with her own: "Have they rearranged the work units then? To keep the factory going?" Maria shrugs. "Change of plan," she says. "Another train has arrived from the East."

PART I

For storytelling is always the art of repeating stories, and this art is lost when the stories are no longer retained. It is lost because there is no more weaving and spinning to go on while they are being listened to. The more self-forgetful the listener is, the more deeply is what he listens to impressed upon his memory. When the rhythm of work has seized him, he listens to the tales in such a way that the gift of retelling them comes to him all by itself. This, then, is the nature of the web in which the gift of storytelling is cradled.

— WALTER BENJAMIN, *The Storyteller*

Arbeit macht frei
Work sets you free

— NAZI CONCENTRATION CAMP SLOGAN

June 2011
Niagara Falls, Canada

I SIT IN THE COOLNESS OF my grandmother's basement, laptop on the vinyl tablecloth, facing the basement stove. A forty-watt bulb casts shadows on the wooden shelving crowded with jars of pickled beets and marinated banana peppers. Every year, my mother and I make this pilgrimage "back east," leaving the breezes of the Pacific coast for my grandmother's house and the Southern Ontario summer. Every year, I set up this temporary air-conditioned refuge, though when I was a child these visits were marked by better ways of keeping cool: ice cream sandwiches and cherry popsicles and watermelon wedges doled out by my grandmother with an indulgent, almost vengeful satisfaction.

One heatwave, the one that stands out like sun-streaked footage from a home movie, my grandparents bought a plastic wading pool and filled it with water from the garden hose. My three cousins and I — all girls, aged three to seven at the time — threw off our sticky summer sundresses and jumped into the freezing water, our pulses racing as the icy water sloshed over the side and onto the closely cut lawn beneath. This shrieking glee lasted until the neighbour across the way phoned and threatened to call the police, confirming in my young mind that not only was suburban Ontario unimaginably humid, it was also ridiculously prohibitive.

On the small West Coast island my mother and I had come from, it was unusual for young children not to be naked at the beach. During parties, these same children would race through the orchard, climbing trees and picking golden plums from the highest branches until well into the August night. At the annual community salmon barbecue, we would form unsupervised packs, darting among the straw hats of long-time farming residents, the grass-stained sleeping bags of young families, and the patchouli-scented home-dyed fabrics of the Coho Drive contingent, who every year would spin in ecstatic circles to acoustic strumming from the plywood stage.

What my grandparents thought of my parents' move to the coast during the wilds of the seventies, other than it was "far, so far," I really couldn't say. My mother met my father when they were both teaching at a community college in Toronto. When teaching contracts dried up, they drove across the country in an Econoline van to seek their fortune out west. In a copper mining town on northern Vancouver Island, my father, long hair and all, was immediately hired to service the mine's giant Lectra Hauls, those bright yellow monster trucks with their ten-foot tires. My mother drove the trucks he worked on through the hairpin turns between the pit and the refinery — or she did after threatening a lawsuit when all she was offered was secretarial work. This was 1973, after all, and things were changing — to the malicious displeasure of some of the other drivers, one of whom slipped LSD in her coffee before her midnight shift. This disaster in the making was interrupted by a flat tire on her truck which meant she spent the night in the repair shop instead of on the road. The grimy walls of the repair shop were papered in centrefold posters, and my not-yet mother, twenty-three at the time, leaned against one of the giant tires until dawn, breathing in the distinctive odours of rubber, oil grease, and sweat, watching the models' enormous breasts magnify and retreat.

On the bright side, my parents did make a great deal of money, which they promptly spent flying back and forth between Port Hardy and Vancouver, where restaurants and jazz bars filled the peninsula between the port and the bridges. Eventually conceding they were not cut out for mining life, they found jobs at a small college on central Vancouver Island. On discovering that the best parties were on a still smaller island twenty minutes' ferry ride from their work, they bought a wooded piece of property on its western side, a part of the island invariably and disconcertingly termed "the North End."

Out West: My parents, Lucy and Brian, 1973

When my grandmother first visited my parents' house, with its vaulted wooden ceilings and skylights, a good ten-minute walk through leagues of Douglas fir from the closest neighbour, her only comment was that the windows would benefit from some nice lace curtains, a suggestion my mother has declined to act on for over three decades.

My grandmother's preoccupation with lace has its own history, rooted in a bone-deep belief that lace symbolizes the triumph of civilization over barbarism, beauty over the brutal ugliness of poverty. As one who travelled from the fields of Stalin-starved Ukraine to a forced labour camp in Hitler's Germany, through DP camps to post-war Canada, she would know. Lace is everywhere in my grandmother's house — the curtains, the doilies, the dining room tablecloth. It is meant to be a barrier.

As for me — someone who documents twentieth-century literary history for a living — I spend a lot of time in libraries and archives and similarly quiet, dimly lit places. Coming from a line of women who travelled far, so far, to get where they are, you might ask why I would choose this particular life. I can only speculate that born as I was at the western limit of the western coast, the only place to go was back.

I tell you all this because I have become convinced that these movements, like overlapping flight routes in the in-flight magazine of the Boeing 767 that brought my mother and me here, are central to what happened next. All of it — the refugee swell out of the ruins of Europe; the postwar affluence; the restless sense of personal destiny of the sixties and seventies; the more ironic and often less expansive life path forged by my own generation, we strangely acquiescent captives of the millennium — led us to this point: to me among the pickled beets, my mother and grandmother in the kitchen above organizing final details for entertaining the family the following weekend.

At the time, I was oblivious to most of this. The name Elsie Kühn-Leitz meant little to me, just a woman my grandmother had worked for during the war. I am intent on starting some new project, as I have recently finished an article on the American poet Charles Olson. Olson spent part of the early fifties wandering the Yucatan, disillusioned by World War II, digging up the Mayan past with a shovel, looking for a remnant that might lead to a more hopeful future. It was an adventurous, physical endeavour and I admire it. I am looking for a new project and consider Mina Loy, a British heroine of inter-war modernism who briefly joined up with a gang of avant-garde radicals called the Italian Futurists whose major objective was to blow up the past and glorify the great technological future. Loy harnessed the Futurists' energy and bombast, had affairs with both of the movement's leaders, subverted their aggressive aesthetics for her own artistic purposes, and promptly set off for inter-war New York. There is a lot to like in this and I scan an academic database, searching for a place to start.

It is possible that the argument upstairs had been going on for some time, dulled by the floor between us and the hum of air conditioning. But it was in this moment that I became aware of my mother and grandmother's voices.

"Mom, what's this?"

"What's what?" A strained innocence from my grandmother.

"This bowl in the refrigerator."

"Oh, Lucy, you know. That just little bit meat for meat on stick."

"But we agreed I would make lasagna."

"Lucy, listen. Laurie and Jerry drive all way from Rochester to see us. Your brother drive across border from Lewiston. And no meat on a stick? No vareniki?"

"Mom, those Ukrainian foods are too much work. Too hard on your back."

"Not so hard. I make only some."

"You'll make a mountain. I know you. Let me make the lasagna. Something in one dish."

"They drive so far to see us and you make only one dish?"

"I only mean it will be easier."

"Jerry like meat on stick. Always his favourite."

"Yes, and he'll like lasagna, too. And so will Laurie."

"I know Laurie since she five years old. In DP camp. She almost seventy now. Can't believe."

"I know, Mom."

"You and Sasha only visit me once a year. Who knows what happen next year? Terrible, terrible thing happen sometime."

The electricity of this exchange transmits itself on a current of cool air, causing me to look for my brown suitcase pressed in beside a stack of white plastic lawn chairs. I get up and nab a gift bag from the otherwise empty suitcase. My bare feet slap on the linoleum as I carefully hurry up the three stairs to the rec room, up another level to the back door, and one more short flight into the upstairs kitchen. The air is filled with the incriminating scent of garlic.

Light streams over the sink through the kitchen's south-facing window, hitting the framed print of *The Last Supper* that hangs over the kitchen table. My mother and grandmother stand at opposite sides of the kitchen, not more than four feet apart, my grandmother in front of the white fridge, my mother beside the cabinets with the peek-a-boo view into the dining room beyond. My grandmother clutches a giant aluminum bowl of marinating meat cubes to her white lace blouse, a light blue scarf tied around her grey curls. My mother, sixty and looking all of forty, leans against the oven, her shoulder-length blonde hair spilling across her Harley Davidson t-shirt, which in turn brushes the top of fitted black jeans. In her right hand, she holds the box of lasagna noodles, and I can see her nails digging into the cardboard. I try inserting something into the moat of exasperation.

"Baba, I got you something," I say, holding out the bag. My grandmother places the bowl protectively on the counter behind her and wipes her hands with a dishcloth.

"What is, Sasha?"

She accepts the bag and pulls out a gauzy peach-coloured scarf with lace edges, rubs the material between her thumb and forefinger, feeling for quality.

"Beautiful," she murmurs. "Thank you, Sashinka."

"Will you wear it to church?" I ask, knowing this is the ultimate venue for compliment exchange, the give and take of family trophies.

"Oh, no," she says softly. "Too special. I put with my outfit."

"Your outfit? For the lunch this weekend?"

"No. Come with me. You too, Lucy."

"This discussion isn't over, Mom," my mother says, tossing the box of lasagna noodles on the stovetop. "You never understand when things are too much. Lyudini nye machini."

This last line, "people are not machines" is something my grandmother likes to say to other people. She waves her hand dismissively and
leads us up the cream-carpeted stairs to the bedrooms. Because we are
following her, and only because we are following her, my grandmother
pointedly uses the hand railing. The wall surfaces of the stairwell are
crowded with photographs — the grandkids as children, my grandfather in his sixties sitting on a giant slide at the downtown amusement
park, my mother and uncle Alex as teenagers, all blue jeans and cheekbones. At the end of the hall, my grandmother turns into her talc-scented
bedroom. She moves toward the closet and my mother and I sit on the
far side of the bed, the side my grandmother still sleeps on, turning to
the closet doors. The peach bedspread is smooth under my hand, quilted
sateen, bought on sale at The Bay or Eaton's.

"You know where is, Lucy?" my grandmother asks, pulling on
one of the closet's mirrored sliding doors. "My special outfit. Always
on left side my closet." She pulls a cream-coloured linen dress off the
rack. The dress hangs neatly on a wooden hanger underneath a clear
plastic dry-cleaning bag. My grandmother presses the scarf against the
plastic, examining the outfit critically for a moment.

"Yes, perfect. See, I know."

"Are you going to a wedding?" I ask.

"No," she says, pleased. "This is outfit I buried in. Scarf look nice
in coffin. Matches material I pick out for lining."

I wait for the punchline, but my grandmother is in earnest, the
intelligent, hawkish cast of her profile intent on the assessment of her
ensemble.

"Open coffin in Ukrainian church, you know, Sasha. Need to look
good."

My grandmother smooths an invisible wrinkle under the bag.
Satisfied, she puts the dress back in the closet. Next, she carefully folds
the scarf and places it on the hat shelf above the dress.

"Be so nice," my grandmother says with a sigh, her back still
turned. "Be so nice to make big lunch with you and Sasha, Lucy . . .
one last time."

I see my mother's mouth twitch, the hint of an eye roll.

"Mom, you've been saying that for thirty years."

My grandmother chuckles, turns to face us. "But every year could be true!"

"Mom —"

"No. It's okay — you don't want to make lunch all together —"

"Mom —"

"All special foods . . ."

"Mom, we made a plan —"

"So, plan change, Lucy. Plan in life change all time. Look at me, graduated as schoolteacher in Kiev. But then war come, I bury my teaching certificate under pear tree in village at home, German plane bomb tree — poof! No more teaching certificate. So, lunch menu change. That not such big change to plan."

My mother shakes her head, knowing she has been had, and so easily. My grandmother smiles then, and her dark eyes are mischievous and triumphant.

"You do good job, Sasha," my grandmother says, moving around the corner of the bed to pat my cheek. As she turns, she is framed in the closet mirror by the leaves of the birch trees outside the bedroom window. In most ways, the shift is unremarkable: a brightening of the light, a sudden greenness, a foreign field.

June 1942
Wetzlar, Germany

THE GROUND SEEMS TO RISE AND fall in an uncertain rhythm as Irina and the others are ordered out of the train cars and marched to a wire enclosure. In a confined cement area with other young women, Irina is ordered to strip. The girls and women are pushed into a disinfection area, pesticide showers, before being issued temporary shift dresses, clogs, and white and blue badges with the letters OST printed in the centre.

In a central assembly area, a guard, starched in his tailored uniform, barks sentences in German. A tall blonde woman with startling blue eyes stands beside him. She introduces herself in Ukrainian as Maria Holliwata, the camp liaison. When the guard speaks again, Maria translates: They are now Ostarbeiter, Eastern workers. They will work for the glory of Hitler and the German people. Those who try to escape will be found. Those who do not work will be shot. After this orientation, the women are divided into metal-roofed barracks. Irina is assigned to a room with seven others, none from her village.

At four-thirty the next morning, the women are roused, given fifteen minutes to wash in the communal latrines, and issued a cup of water and a small piece of dark, dry bread. The labourers are then marched a half-mile down the road. As they walk, Irina comes to understand the clogs. The clomping of their heels on the ground is as identifiable as a cow with a bell. The guards march the prisoners to one of two modern buildings, ten stories tall with a stern modern façade. Their building has the name Ernst Leitz written at the top in large, illuminated letters, bright in the dawn light. The women are divided into work units and given protective clothing. Irina is assigned to an assembly line where glass lenses are packed into cardboard boxes and then into plain wooden crates. The factory smells of nothing in particular, only a numbing efficiency. Every day, Irina stands beside the other women and packs ten lenses to a box, twelve boxes to a crate. The crates are made of a light wood. The repetitive activity and cool glass are a comfort.

The first week, Irina keeps her eyes down, looking at nothing but the glass lenses, the cardboard boxes, the wooden crates. Later she watches the overseer as he strides along the rows of working women, snapping at a misstep or inefficiency.

Irina spends three months packing lenses in the factory, days marked by turnip soup, the contractions of hunger pain, and cool, airless work in the factory. At night, in the half-hour before the harsh overhead light goes out, she reads her translation dictionary and learns new words in German: *unterwasser, gefühl, Flucht.* She tries to think in sentences that take in more than what is immediately in front of her, but her brain feels stilted, stunned into emotionless observation: *the dictionary, the metal bed frame, the fence.*

One morning the overseer, a stout, grey-haired man in his fifties who spends his time peering over the shoulders of the women, standing too close, stops behind her. "Why are you packing eight lenses to a box instead of ten?" he asks roughly. He moves to pick up the box and show her what he means but Irina responds:

"Because the boxes that arrived this morning are smaller, sir," she says. She has been waiting for this moment to use her German and is satisfied by the startled look on the overseer's face. He removes his glasses, polishes them with a small blue cloth, replaces them on his nose, looks at her again.

"Where did you learn German?"

"In school, sir."

Two days later, Irina is transferred to work in the camp hospital under a German doctor named Braun. She and several other German-speaking Ukrainian women translate between doctor and camp patients, wash and bandage wounds, and keep the facility clean. Sometimes the patients are the youngest workers in the camp, the thirteen- and fourteen-year-olds who suffer most from malnutrition. Other days, Irina tends to the newly interned who have been sprayed with the acid-based disinfectant that leaves large red burns on their backs, chests, and legs. One day she holds the hand of a woman giving birth. "Get it out, get it out," the woman screams. "It's German. Get it out of me. My baby. Where is my baby?" Sometimes, at the end of day, Irina stands at the edge of the camp and looks out into the fields. The fields are endless and look like home.

June 2011
Niagara Falls, Canada

THE BOWL OF MARINATING MEAT, still cold from the fridge, sits in the centre of the kitchen table. Its outside surface, warming in the light humidity of the kitchen, is covered in condensation. Inside the bowl, the one-inch cubes of pork and beef marinate in garlic, evaporated milk, and egg. "Meat on stick" is originally a Cossack dish, though my grandmother substitutes satay sticks for swords, as well as other concessions to the suburban kitchen: the skewers are rolled in Shake 'n Bake, fried until the coating is dark and crispy, and simmered in the oven in bouillon until soft.

Despite her arthritic fingers, my grandmother is nimble at spearing the meat, knitting the skewer in and out of the folds of each cube, alternating between the beef and pork. She radiates proficiency, sure in the knowledge that this ongoing repetition of small movements will lead directly to the happiness of others. She visibly gains strength as a row of completed skewers grows on the plate beside her. My mother, checking her initial reluctance, is quick and determined. On the third side of the table, I do my best to keep a skewer straight in spearing through the eggy slipperiness of the meat.

From the unusually long silence, I can tell my grandmother is still thinking about whatever it was that came for her in the bedroom, and my mother is weighing whether she should ask about it. My grandmother's recounting of the past, like her recipes, is set, but occasionally something will fall out in the telling, some previously unmentioned ingredient that is key to all the rest. It is not that she has hidden her past — not its broad outlines, at least — but that she tends to repeat the same stock stories, her words almost identical each time. Things she would never have told us before have become more common since her eighty-eighth birthday in December. Knowing this, my mother takes a breath, presses her hip against the table, makes her voice light.

"So — tell us something."

For a moment the kitchen is silent except for the hum of the fridge, the clicking of our fingernails against the sides of the metal bowl, the low thrum of a car accelerating toward the neighbourhood park down the road.

"Tell you what?" my grandmother says, impatient, set on her task.

My mother keeps working, deliberately keeping her eyes on the skewer in front of her. "Tell us something about the war."

My grandmother sniffs. "War was bad time. You lucky to be living now." She places a finished skewer on the plate. "Later, Lucy, I want you cut my hair a little bit, please. Hairdresser does bad job this time — sticking out funny on left side."

She raises a hand to touch the curls under her headscarf but then, remembering the egginess of her fingers, lowers her hand.

"Used to be Tiffany cut my hair. She do good job. Always set curls very nice. But she have baby and now this Ashley in salon in mall don't care how it turn out. All the time she do my hair she telling me about boyfriend in St. Catharines and how he take her to Céline Dion concert in Toronto. She no pay attention! I pay her twenty-five dollar and look like crazy lady when I come out."

For a moment, my grandmother is completely absorbed by this tale, her lips pursed in indignation, playing the scene at the hairdresser over in her mind. When she sighs, I think we are going to hear more about Ashley. But whatever it was that appeared in the bedroom is still lingering, and then there is the rhythm of our work. My grandmother sighs again, as though wearied by the silence.

"You know we have no meat at home," she says, the texture of the meat against her fingertips seeming to summon the memory of its absence. "I no learn to make meat on stick until we leave DP camp with other Ukrainian and Russian people and live in Belgium on way to Canada."

My mother and I keep skewering, allowing the quiet to do its work.

"In Ukraine, maybe some fish and nuts at Christmas. When Germans come, Collective put out embroidered tablecloth with bread and salt, traditional welcome. We think maybe Germans save us from Stalin, from terrible hunger. Stalin hate Ukrainians, try to starve us to death, and we hungry all time. Lady who lived next door to us in village so hungry she go crazy and eat her own children. When we kids, Mama no let us out at night in case someone steal us for meat. But Germans take all young people in trains to work camp in Germany. They have food but they give us so little, enough to keep working."

"You know, too, that I lucky. Lots of people suffer in work camp. Make what happen to me like some kind miracle."

September, 1942
Wetzlar, Germany

ONE MORNING, A WOMAN IN HER late thirties enters the camp hospital. She is dressed in a soft camel hair coat, her dark-blonde hair smoothed back into two buns which sit just below her ears. Her manner is calm and considered. Doctor Braun speaks with her in low, respectful tones. Quietly, the woman makes her way around the medical clinic, speaking in German to each of the Eastern European hospital workers, each of whom responds in the same. Irina is rolling bandages in the corner of the clinic when the woman approaches her.

"You are making quick work of that," the woman says. "Quicker than my children could unroll them, which is saying something."

"They are used up very quickly, gnädige Frau."

"What is your name?" the woman asks.

"Irina Kylynych."

"I am Elsie Kühn-Leitz. You may call me Frau Elsie, Irina."

The woman smiles and gently squeezes Irina's arm before moving on and Irina smells her perfume, the light scent of lilies, which quickly dissipates into the antiseptic smell of the clinic. When Frau Elsie has finished touring the room, she and the doctor speak briefly in the corner by the medical supply cabinet. Frau Elsie then steps out of the clinic into the barren yard beyond.

Doctor Braun nods. "Marina, Irina, Leah," he says, his voice clipped.

Irina puts down the bandages and approaches the doctor along with Marina, a stocky, dark-haired woman from Odesa, and Leah, a taller redhead from outside Kyiv.

"Frau Kühn-Leitz has chosen the three of you to work at Haus Friedwart, her family's home on the hill." Doctor Braun turns, his beard short and angular in profile against the leanness of his face. "The Leitz family is very important," he adds unnecessarily. "Do not make any mistakes."

The doctor gestures to the door and the three women walk into the yard. A guard appears in an open-backed truck and takes them to the barracks to collect their few things. When they return, Frau Elsie is standing in the yard talking with Maria Holliwata, the camp liaison. Irina watches the exchange with curiosity. They are clearly friendly, their heads bent together. Though never to her face, the other women in Irina's room refer to the liaison as Maria Holy Water, imitate her imperiousness, the capriciousness of her favour, soap and extra rations for those who do her bidding. When Elsie sees Irina, Marina, and Leah approaching, she pats Maria's arm much in the way she had Irina's and turns to the three nervous women.

"You're ready? Come with me," she says.

They follow Frau Elsie to the guard post at the end of the yard, where she hands papers to the guard. The guard scans each of the women but lets them pass. Beyond the guard station, a tall, older man in a dark uniform, non-military, is waiting beside a large black car. As the women emerge from the camp, he gently takes their belongings and puts them in the trunk. He opens the front door for Frau Elsie, who slips into the passenger seat, and the backseat door for the other women. Irina hesitates, then leads the others onto the soft black leather seat. Leah and Marina press in beside her. They too seem to be holding their breath, Marina fussing with a white spot on her blue uniform left by the hospital disinfectant. Frau Elsie turns to face them. She is more at ease inside the car, her arm resting on the leather seat.

"I chose the three of you because you have the best German," Frau Elsie says, "and it's about personality, too, isn't it? We need women to help in the house, and I hope you will be comfortable. Friedrich will vouch for us."

In profile, the chauffeur smiles slightly and nods as the car pulls out of the road leading from the camp into the town. This is the first time Irina has seen Wetzlar beyond the camp, the factory, and the stretch of road in between. They drive over a churning river on a handsome stone bridge, through the main street with its white houses trimmed with dark wood. Townspeople walk through the narrow streets in tailored overcoats, collars turned up against the late September chill. Women push babies in buggies, enter bakeries and pharmacies, stop to speak in small groups on the sidewalk.

Sensing her passengers' disorientation, Frau Elsie keeps up a running commentary, pointing out the market area and the church, as well as the ruined Roman towers on the town's outskirts.

"At one time Wetzlar was important for its size. It housed the court of the Holy Roman Empire," Frau Elsie says as the car climbs the steep hill above the town. "When the Empire dissolved in the early eighteen hundreds, there were still almost twenty judges employed by the court. It was a very sophisticated system of law, for its time . . ."

As they near the top of the hill, Friedrich turns toward an elegant white stone villa surrounded by gardens. The car stops in front of an impressive stone staircase, and Frau Elsie says, "Haus Friedwart," before briskly opening her door. The house is unlike anything Irina has seen, as large as the former summer castle of the tsars on the edge of Stanytsia. The surrounding bushes are manicured and flowers grow in tasteful groupings.

Frau Elsie leads Irina, Marina, and Leah up the tawny stone staircase onto a pillared terrace that overlooks the town, river, and the factory. In the entryway, Irina feels dwarfed by the domed ceiling. Embroidered carpets sit at the centre of several of the rooms that branch off the main hallway. There are giant porcelain vases on large oak tables. Frau Elsie explains that the basement contains the cellars, kitchen, one staff room, and a heating room. The ground floor has more rooms for the live-in staff as well as the dining room and reception room. The first floor includes living, music, and breakfast rooms as well as a study and bedroom for Frau Elsie's father, Herr Leitz. Frau Elsie has a suite of rooms on the top floor for herself, her two daughters, and her son.

"My husband is away," she says, taking off her gloves. "Mostly I live here with my father and my children." She concludes by telling them they will receive a few reichsmarks a month in addition to meals and lodging.

After this introduction, Frau Elsie sits down with them in the workers' dining room, for a lunch of venison stew and liverwurst on a light rye bread cut into quarters. Irina cannot recall ever having so much meat at one meal. She watches Frau Elsie eat and tries to take similarly small spoonfuls of stew, to gently dab her mouth with a napkin the way her new employer does. She sees Marina's hand shake and knows that she, too, is resisting the urge to push the sandwich into her mouth before it is taken away. Frau Elsie pretends not to notice and introduces them to the young German woman serving lunch, whose name is Heidi.

After lunch, Frau Elsie encourages the new employees to rest in their rooms. "You will sleep in the room beside Heidi's, Irina. Marina and Leah will sleep in the larger room across the hall. I've left some dresses in the closets for you. Nothing fancy, and they will probably need adjusting. You're all so very thin." She frowns and Irina can see she is about to say something else, but instead she gestures to the rooms and leaves them.

Irina sits on the single bed in the room that has been assigned to her. The room is small but comfortable, furnished with a dresser and wardrobe in the same dark wood as the bed frame. Irina's belongings have been transferred to her room and sit at the end of the bed, one more strange apparition in the series of events that has been the morning.

She stares out the window, the glass clear and flawless. She can see green bushes, a burst of small purple flowers, and a lawn stretching out to the edge of the embankment. An older man, tall and clean-shaven in a brown linen suit and a white hat with a brown band comes into view. He is dressed carefully but walks aimlessly, whacking at weeds in the lawn with some kind of long-handled mallet. Irina guesses this is Ernst Leitz, Frau Elsie's father, whose name is spelled out on the top of the factory. The man stares down the hill for a while, a muscular tension in his stillness, before walking slowly back toward the house.

Irina watches, then stands and gently opens the wardrobe across from the bed. Hanging inside is a maid's uniform like Heidi's, black with a full skirt and white apron. Beside it there is a beige nightgown with long sleeves. At the end of the rack there are two dresses, one grey and one blue. The grey one is made of a soft wool, cut just below the knee, with a finely tailored cloth belt and a tie at the neck. The blue one is lighter and silkier and reminds Irina of the colour of the sky just after sunset in Stanytsia. She pulls the blue dress close to her body and feels the combination of silk and starch against her throat.

"The clothes are all Frau Elsie's," Heidi says from the doorway. Irina is startled but Heidi gives a little motion with her hand to indicate she shouldn't worry. "She gives them to us once she's worn them for a season or two."

"How long have you worked here?" Irina asks, putting the dress back in the closet. Even though these clothes are now hers she feels she has been caught touching something she shouldn't.

"Four years. Not as long as some, though I'm not as old either! Still, I was here before the war. You should have seen the parties then. Champagne and music and dancing. Writers, artists, businessmen and their wives. Everything is different now, of course."

Irina does not know what to say to this. She smooths the bed-spread. *Her bed*, she says cautiously to herself.

Heidi looks at her with curiousity. "You aren't really resting, are you?"

Irina shakes her head.

"Then come on. I'll show you more of the house. And Frau Elsie wants you to serve dinner on Sundays so I'll teach you that, too. I'll bet you've never seen this kind of table setting."

Irina hurries to follow Heidi down to the kitchen. On her left, she can see three women working, one doing dishes, one peeling potatoes, and one, the heftiest, looking critically at a rump roast in a large pan. Heidi gives a half-wave and the woman peeling potatoes nods before turning back to her task. Heidi points out the cellars, explaining how they are organized before leading Irina back up to the ground floor, then up a wood-panelled staircase to what she calls the first floor, gesturing to a music room with powder-blue walls and rose curtains, the living room with its plush embroidered carpet in pink and green with groupings of chairs and couches. Each room has enormous windows with views of the gardens or the town. Though the afternoon is overcast, the house is full of light.

They pass a room with its door half closed and Heidi says in a low voice, "Herr Leitz's study. He is over seventy now but still busy, here in Wetzlar but also with Leica production at the foreign offices, the ones in New York and London and so on. Sometimes Herr Leitz sends employees overseas, but only the ones from the factory, not us in the house. Too bad! New York City — can you imagine?"

Heidi leads the way up to Frau Elsie's floor. The carpet is a light rose here, and the decorations seem to reflect Frau Elsie — solid, sturdy couches and lamps with delicate floral designs on porcelain bases. They pass the children's playroom, lined with a shelf of stuffed animals and dolls from across Europe. Irina recognizes a doll in full Bavarian costume, a porcelain Pierrot from France, and a wooden matryoshka doll, beautifully painted and lacquered. On the floor, an elaborate miniature train set claims one end of the room. Sitting on the carpet at the other end, a blonde girl of about four plays with a stuffed rabbit under the supervision of a governess. As the little girl looks up, her eyelids flutter slowly. The look in her green eyes is distant. She is a beautiful child, with blonde hair and glossy pink lips.

"Frau Elsie's youngest, Karin," Heidi says. She makes no further comment until they reach a suite of bedrooms, which Heidi says belong to Frau Elsie and her two older children, Knut and Cornelia. There are portraits of the three children and Irina notes how handsome they are, all within a year or two of each other, all with straight teeth and good skin.

The women take the stairs back down to the ground floor, where Heidi ends the tour with the formal dining room. The table is covered by a finely patterned lace cloth and framed by ten chairs with black leather backs. A painting of a lake with pine trees and mountains in the background hangs over the sideboard, from which Heidi removes a dark box. From the glass cabinet on the other side of the room, she takes down some gold-plated dishes. Slowly, so Irina can follow, she removes the silverware from the box and lays a setting at the head of the table: napkin, dinner fork, salad fork to the left of the plate; salad knife, dinner knife, soup spoon, teaspoon on the right; dessert fork and coffee spoon above the plate, facing opposite directions; bread plate with butter knife on the top left.

"Just like that, each time," Heidi says. "Have you got it?"

"I think so," Irina says, wondering how so many pieces of cutlery are necessary.

"Good. Sundays are my day off and Frau Elsie will expect you to set and serve on your own. Remember, always serve from the left, clear from the right, except side dishes and bread. Understand?"

Irina nods, but she is not sure. She studies the table setting, trying to memorize its details.

That night, Irina lies in bed, the long sleeves of the night-gown sitting strangely on her skin. The lack of sound is uncanny. For months she has listened to camp noises, the restlessness of the women, the shouts of the Gestapo sentries, the barking of dogs, the intermittent screams of men or women who have been taken out into the yard, the sobs of teenage girls. Before that she slept in the dormitory of the college in Kyiv. Others would come and go late into the night while she studied or worried that her grades would not be high enough, that her scholarship would be lost, that she would never be a teacher. Before that she slept in straw on the floor of one room with her five siblings, lulled by the low tones or exhausted sighs of her parents that would seep under the door that separated them. Each of these rooms seems to sit inside the next, making her vision sway in the darkness. To settle herself, Irina counts pieces of silverware in her head: salad fork, dinner fork, soup spoon, knife. These are her new lessons, the geometry of salvation, however temporary.

Haus Friedwart

(SOURCE: ERNST LEITZ FOUNDATION)

June 2011
Niagara Falls, Canada

MY GRANDMOTHER FRIES THE MEAT ON sticks in the basement, in the second kitchen my grandfather built for her when they bought this house. As the skewers brown, the scent spreads through the house, reminding me of childhood visits where my cousins and I would gather around a table heaped with mashed potatoes, creamed spinach, and a platter of meat on sticks at the centre. There has never been any question about the way my grandmother values meat, of its centrality to the economy of staying alive. Teenage bouts of vegetarianism were viewed with the same incomprehension as our wardrobes, the choice of ripped jeans when whole ones were available, tank tops when there were pretty blouses, the thong she once pulled out of the dryer when my cousins were visiting. "But Sasha," she said, her eyes wide. "This *stripper* underwear!"

My grandmother fries and I tap idly at my computer. Perhaps because it belongs so thoroughly to this house, it has never occurred to me to research my grandmother's past. But now, the stories of the morning and the lull in my own work cause me to type "Leica" into Google. A line of antique and modern camera images appears at the top of the page. Below this, there is a site about the current Leica factory in Wetzlar, which boasts an interactive museum and a hotel. There are fan sites devoted to the cameras themselves with elaborate diagrams of the camera's evolution.

Danish photographer and Leica enthusiast Thorsten Overgaard provides a history of the company. I learn that the Leitz operation was not always devoted to camera-making. At the turn of the century, Ernst Leitz Optical Industry mostly produced high-quality microscopes and hunting scopes. The Leica name was spliced together from the first three letters of the name *Leitz* and the first two letters of the word *camera*. The first prototype was devised in 1913 by Oskar Barnack, a Leitz employee head-hunted by Elsie's grandfather, Ernst Leitz I, after whom the company was named.

Barnack had no set job. He was encouraged to research, experiment, and follow his interests, which included developing cameras for moving pictures. Barnack's eureka moment was the idea of using small negatives to create larger pictures. This was the breakthrough that ended the era of large-format box cameras on stationary tripods. A Leitz optical designer named Max Berek devised the 50 mm lens, Leica's standard lens to this day.

Ernst Leitz II, Elsie's father, took over the company in 1920 and it was his 1924 decision to make Leicas for a consumer market. The cameras were high quality and expensive but they gained an early following among artists and journalists who valued the candid possibilities of the new portability. Adopters included Henri Cartier-Bresson, a sometimes visitor to Haus Friedwart; Robert Capa; and later, Annie Lebovitz. I learn the Leica is the camera behind some of the most iconic war imagery of the twentieth century: Capa's Spanish Civil War photos, Eisenstaedt's nurse and sailor kissing in Times Square, Ut's naked girl running from napalm.

I look up from the screen. In front of me, my grandmother continues her preparations for Saturday's lunch. Ambition was never her problem, and if she is favouring her left leg, it is probably because she pulled out both refrigerators to clean underneath before our arrival. I survey the pantry of carefully stacked canned and boxed foods. I look back at the screen, watching the way the pixilation creates swirls against the background. Restless, I move over to the stove, scrounging for scraps, the little brown pieces of fried Shake 'n Bake that have fallen off the skewers that my grandmother puts on a salad plate beside the stove. My grandmother shifts slightly to the right to make room for me.

"I don't mean disturb your work, Sasha."

"You're not disturbing me. Anyway, it's your house. We're disturbing you."

"You never disturb me. I be so lucky be so disturb every day. But if you no working, you watch. Maybe you make meat on stick for John." She eyes my waistline, thickened by the fifth month of pregnancy. "So nice last year you finally get married. And now this year baby. Maybe you have nice dinner party, make meat on stick. Important in good life, you know."

I do know. The dinner table, or preparing for the table, has been central to most of the contentment I have felt and most of the stories that I know. But it is also strangely far from the life I live now, reflected in the bright but empty comments of real estate agents on the occasions John and I have ventured out to look at bigger apartments on Vancouver's vertiginous real estate market: "Here's the kitchen, compact of course . . . and the living room. No space for a formal dining room in new builds. It's not part of the *lifestyle culture* to entertain like that anymore . . ."

For about ten seconds, I consider trying to explain this to my grandmother.

"Don't wrinkle your forehead, Sasha. Bad for wrinkles. I know, yes? Every day I put on Oil of Olay twice a day but still wrinkles. Oh well. I old woman. I earn it. But you . . . You pay attention, you watch. Everything be okay for you."

My grandmother moves some of the darkened skewers to the sides of the skillet and shuffles the lighter ones around the edges toward the middle. Seeing the centre of the skillet is dry, she adds a knife's edge of butter that liquifies and bubbles. As the vapour rises from the pan, she turns up the stove fan. The fan makes a rhythmic whirring sound over the crackling of the butter.

"So nice to have downstairs kitchen for frying," my grandmother says. And then, as though it is a continuation of the same thought: "Kitchen in Leitz house was downstairs. Kitchen green, too, like my stove. But that house, Sasha, was mansion. Like palace it was for me."

September 1942
Wetzlar, Germany

HER FIRST MORNING AT HAUS FRIEDWART, Irina wakes early. She watches the light spread across the lawn until it reaches the garden statue of a man holding a feather, which seems to ignite the day. She hears Heidi stirring in the next room, pots being moved on the stove in the kitchen downstairs. Irina dresses in her maid's uniform and washes in the servants' bathroom with its porcelain sink and etched fixtures, so different from the communal latrines of the camp. The staff then report to Frau Vogel, the housekeeper, over a breakfast of coffee and sweet rolls. The glaze on the sweet rolls shines under the overhead light in the kitchen, and Irina has to check the impulse not to grab several rolls and stuff them in the pockets of her uniform. Heidi tells Irina to help herself to coffee, which Irina has never had before.

"Enjoy it while it lasts," Heidi says, pulling a mournful face. "We're getting to the last of what Frau Lichen put in storage before the war. Soon it will be roasted barley, like everywhere else. For now, we still have sugar, though."

Irina fixes her coffee as Heidi does, with milk and a little of the sugar. The liquid is hot, sweet and bitter at once, and the dim room seems to take on a muted glow as Irina drinks it. She nods at Leah and Marina, also wearing their black maid's dresses, and Marina smiles back. Leah, pale in her black uniform, looks stunned.

Frau Vogel, tall with grey hair pulled back, sits at the head of the long table, several pieces of paper in front of her. She tells Leah and Marina they will be working with an older housekeeper named Ada that day, dusting, washing the marble entryway, and polishing the silver. Irina would like to polish the silver, too, to have another day to learn its secrets, but instead she is told she will do the daily marketing.

"See Friedrich in the garage," Frau Vogel says. She is in her early sixties, self-assured, solid in the full authority of the house. "He will find you a bicycle to ride down to the market. I have written out a list. Can you read?"

At first Irina is stung, unsure if, like the camp guards, this woman believes she is stupid and illiterate. But then she realizes that Frau Vogel leaves nothing to chance, probing every angle of the day to make sure it ends squarely where it needs to.

"I read," Irina says.

"Good. The list and the ration stamps are in this envelope. I have counted out the stamps. Make sure the meat is fresh. The vendors won't recognize you so tell them you are shopping for the Leitzes."

Frau Vogel proceeds to give detailed instructions to the rest of the domestic staff, then adjourns the meeting with a wave of her hand. The staff take their dishes to the kitchen sink and proceed with their tasks. Irina holds firmly to the list and envelope from Frau Vogel and walks out to the garage area, where Friedrich is polishing the interior of the black car. When he catches sight of Irina through the windshield, he backs out of the front seat and straightens his long frame.

Irina stands awkwardly for a moment. More than anyone else in the house, Friedrich knows that she has just been fished out of the camp. Friedrich looks at her wryly, pushing his shirtsleeves up over lean, age-spotted forearms. "You have the look of someone sent by

Frau Vogel." He laughs then and says to Irina: "That woman! The Nazis would have won already if she were in charge. What can I do for you?"

"A bicycle? I am supposed to go to the market."

"Movement in the ranks," he murmurs and walks into the garage, emerging with an upright black bicycle with a large wooden basket attached to the handlebars.

"Market's straight down the hill, in the centre of town," Friedrich says. "Stores are on the main street, and the farmers bring their vegetables in to sell in the main square. Even with the rationing, you should be able to get what you need."

Friedrich adjusts the bicycle seat to accommodate Irina's long legs, then pushes the handlebars in her direction. Irina takes the bicycle but continues to stand, unsure of what to do next. Friedrich cocks his head toward the hill.

"Enjoy the way down. You'll have your work cut out for you on the way up."

Irina tucks the list and the envelope in the waistband of her skirt and takes the bicycle from Friedrich, murmuring her thanks. He makes a kind of good-luck clucking noise and returns to the task of polishing the car.

Irina stands there for a moment, the bicycle seat against her hip. It is the freest she has been in months. Where could she go, if she wanted to? How far could she get before someone stopped her? She pushes the thought from her mind. She has no appetite for wandering the wilderness until the Gestapo tracks her down. Instead, she gets on the bicycle and slowly finds her balance as she pushes the pedals down the winding driveway. Her sister, Anya, had a bicycle in the village, given to her by the Collective for delivering letters, almost always pre-opened by the officials. Irina tries not to think of Anya or even the letters, but rather, when she was allowed to ride the bicycle on the dirt path by their house, the way her legs felt as if they were ploughing through the sky. The bicycle swerves a little to the right toward the conifers that line the drive, but Irina rights the handlebars and finds her momentum.

As Irina turns onto the main road, she can see the town spread out before her, the river churning in the distance, the houses becoming gradually less imposing as she descends the hill. Irina follows the road, the breeze teasing her face and skirt. She allows herself a little more speed down a straight section of the hill. She hears a noise and quickly applies the brake, but then realizes it came from her own throat, something between a crow and a laugh. She sets off again, then slows and dismounts, smoothing her skirt, as she reaches the shops of the main street. She pauses, takes a breath, then consults Frau Vogel's list.

The first shop is a bakery. Irina sets her bicycle against the storefront and walks inside, taking a place behind the other shoppers. As she stands in line, she forms the words in her mouth, willing them to come out the way she hears them from the customers ahead of her — clear, precise, bored or authoritative — without the shushing Slavic accent that blurs the contours of German words. When she reaches the front of the line, a middle-aged blonde woman asks what she needs. Irina's lips purse involuntarily and for a moment she thinks the words won't come. The woman looks at her impatiently and Irina presses her tongue forward.

"Two loaves of rye bread," she says.

The woman fetches two crusty oblongs from the wooden shelf behind the counter. "And?"

"One dozen sweet rolls, one dozen dinner rolls." She pauses and then adds, "For the Leitzes." The woman looks up at her, then chooses from the larger buns at the back of a baking sheet. The woman hands Irina her purchases wrapped in brown paper and takes the purple ration stamps with the eagle and swastika suspended above the word *Brot*.

Irina returns to her bicycle and places the packages in the basket. She is passing, if not as German, then as something acceptable, someone who can buy bread in a German store, who is allowed to ride a bicycle in a German street. From the bakery, she makes her way to the butcher and from the butcher to the greengrocer, the Leitz name leading to larger pieces of meat, an extra bit of cheese. As Friedrich said, the farmers have set up a market in the main square, and after gathering most of the purchases from the list, she proceeds among the stalls to pick up the remaining fruit and vegetables on the list. Though the basket is heavy, she knows she can pack a few more items in along the sides. She buys some small red apples at one stand and a dozen eggs from another farmer, a man with rough hands and quick manner. As she is leaving, she checks the eggs to make sure none are cracked and the man scans the OST badge pinned to her coat.

"What are you looking at, you filthy Bolshevik? You think I'm cheating you?"

For a moment Irina thinks he is going to strike the package from her hands.

"No, the eggs. They're for the Leitzes."

"They're for the Leitzes," he imitates. "I'll tell *you* something. That family won't hang on to all those pretty advantages forever, fooling around with Bolsheviks and Jews. I'll tell you."

The farmer takes an aggressive step toward her. Irina looks around, but the man who sold her the apples is studiously counting the bills in his money belt, and a woman sitting on a stool nearby is smirking. Irina hurries away, retrieves her bicycle, and walks swiftly back to the main street.

Irina can feel her pulse skipping, and the eggs tremble as she arranges them carefully on the top of the basket, making sure that the heavier purchases are not pressing on the sweet rolls. She takes a breath and gets on the bicycle, heading back up the hill. It feels good to push something, to move it according to her will. She peddles harder as the hill becomes steeper. Halfway up she is out of breath and has to get off the bicycle and push.

When she reaches the house, Irina takes the bicycle around to the kitchen entrance. The cook, Frau Lichen, is stirring apple cider in a large pot, her broad face flushed and soft from the rising steam. The older woman looks up as Irina comes in and gestures toward a table at the far end of the kitchen. Frau Vogel walks in, consulting her papers.

"Did you get everything?" she asks briskly.

"Yes, Frau Vogel," Irina says, removing the envelope from her waistband. Frau Vogel checks the contents of the envelope, gives a nod, and looks up at Irina.

"How was it?"

"It was fine." Even with the unpleasant incident, she would rather shop ten times a day than return to the camp. In any event, Irina can tell this is the only answer Frau Vogel is interested in hearing.

"Good," Frau Vogel says. "You will do the marketing on a daily basis, except Saturdays, which will be your day off, and Sundays when the shops are closed, and you will serve. After the market, your time is your own until lunch. After lunch, you will help with the dusting."

Irina nods and Frau Vogel turns to Frau Lichen to discuss a small dinner party the Leitzes are hosting the following Tuesday.

On Sunday, the house is quiet. The family goes to church in the morning and lingers afterward. Irina attends the service and floats, for a while, on the melodies sung by the boys' choir. She hurries back to the house when the service ends. Taking advantage of much of the staff's day off and the absence of the family, Irina sets the table carefully: plate, salad fork, dinner fork, knife. Irina is careful to position everything just as it should be. The china is light in her hands and the silver heavy.

Through the conservatory windows, she sees Friedrich walk around the front of the house with a pair of pruning shears. He is smoking and whistling at once, the smoke rising on a curl of sound she can just barely make out. Frau Lichen is in the kitchen, making a roasted chicken and vegetables from the ingredients Irina collected the day before. Irina can smell the combination of roasting poultry and stuffing that drifts up from the stove below. *Rosmarin*, she says to herself, naming the herb she has only just learned the name for. She is glad not to be shopping today, less because of the man in the market, whom she has avoided, and more because her legs are sore and heavy from the trips up the hill.

When the Leitzes return, it is a pleasant blur of colour and sound. Frau Elsie and Cornelia sing to Karin, who responds with a half-smile, the stuffed rabbit clutched against her green velvet dress. Knut speaks animatedly with Herr Leitz about airplanes, but when he senses his grandfather's distraction he turns to his mother instead, full of questions about engines and propellers. Frau Elsie laughs and tickles Karin at the end of the song, and Irina thinks she looks beautiful, her hair pulled back into a loose bun under a black hat with a short veil that just covers her eyes. "So much for your quiet morning, Irina!" Elsie says as she removes her coat and passes it to Irina, who hangs it carefully in the entry closet.

Lunch passes without incident, despite Irina's nervousness. The family comes to the table, Knut with a new Leica, though Frau Elsie makes him leave it on the sideboard during the meal.

When the family leaves the table, Irina clears it. She does not touch the camera, but she admires it and recognizes the lens as the same type she handled in the factory. The camera is only slightly bigger than a pack of cigarettes, palm-sized, with several knobs and slim silver disks on the top, one with the word *Leica* written in a rounded cursive. She is tempted to pick up the camera, to see how much this tightly engineered invention might weigh, but tidies around it instead.

The rest of the day is quiet. Frau Elsie spends the evening with the children in their suite upstairs, Herr Leitz in his rooms. Around eight, shortly before the rest of the staff are due back, Irina sits on her bed, looking at a few photographs of her own. They were not taken with a Leica, but with a heavy black box on a tripod, the day a travelling photographer came around taking pictures of the villagers for money. In one of the photographs, Irina's mother stands in front of their two-bedroom house, bundled in a winter dress and coat, her head covered by an old scarf. Her face is unsmiling. Irina wishes she could have that scarf with her, some familiar smell or texture.

When the doorbell rings, Irina is unsure what to do, but as she is one of the few staff members in the house, she hurries to the door. She peers out the window beside the door but does not recognize the man on the veranda.

"Good evening," the man says when she opens the door. "I am here to see Herr Leitz."

"Herr Leitz has retired," Irina says carefully. This is the first encounter Irina has had with a visitor and she has no idea how he will see her, whether his eye will turn inward the moment he hears her accent. But the man does not seem to notice.

"Mmm. Yes, I am sorry. But please —"

There is an intensity about this man at odds with the quiet progress of a Sunday evening. Even in the dim light of the veranda, Irina can feel it, his jaw muscles knotted under the skin of his thin, angular chin. There is a small tuft of short grey whiskers that he missed while shaving, and Irina finds herself mesmerized by the way they vibrate gently on his cheek.

"It's all right, Irina. Come in, Herr Muntz." Herr Leitz is standing behind her in the entry hall. Drawn up to his full six feet, perfectly dressed in a grey suit on a Sunday evening, Herr Leitz looks imposing, and Irina thinks the visitor is quite brave to drop by without an appointment. The stranger presses forward through the door, almost before Irina can open it fully. He does not have a coat though the evening is cool.

"The study?" Herr Leitz asks before the man can say anything further.

Muntz nods and the men walk together up the stairs. Irina wonders if she is supposed to offer tea or coffee. She has seen Heidi do this when visitors come to the house. Not wanting the men to wait once she has asked, Irina first goes down to the kitchen and puts on some water to boil. She then makes her way upstairs to inquire.

The door to the study is closed. Irina cannot pick out the words of the men, but she can hear the urgency. A thin bar of light is visible underneath the door and suddenly Irina feels herself on the train, the heat of bodies, the smell of urine and fear. She presses her hand against the wall, unsure if this is an assault of memory or premonition, then turns and treads back down the hall.

When Irina returns to the kitchen, the water is boiling on the stove, little bubbles popping against the surface. Heidi walks into the kitchen through the staff entrance, her face flushed from a day outdoors.

"Is that water for tea? I'd love a cup if you're making it."

Sitting at the head of the green kitchen table, Heidi chats about her family, who live in the nearby town of Lahnau. When the tea is ready, Irina pours it into two teacups, brings them to the table, and sits.

"How was the dinner service?" Heidi asks, breaking off her monologue. "Did you drop anything?"

"No, it was fine."

"What's wrong, Irina? You look a million miles away. Are you homesick?"

"No, I . . ."

Upstairs, the main door opens and closes. Heidi looks up.

"Is there someone here?"

"A visitor for Herr Leitz."

"Was it a woman?" Heidi's eyes are wide with curiosity.

"No, it was a man."

"Well," Heidi says, blowing on her tea. "As long as it's not one of the Leitz Werke employees coming around again. And on a Sunday! It's too much to expect."

Irina sips her tea. Heidi returns to chatting about her sister's upcoming wedding to an official in Lahnau.

That night Irina lies on her bed, watching grey clouds float across the surface of the moon. This past week, the walls of this house seemed impenetrable, but now they seem brittle, less resistant. Irina falls into a half-sleep and dreams water the colour of gunmetal is rushing through the windows and doors of Haus Friedwart. She tries to open the front door, but the weight of the water prevents it. She sees something floating past her and grabs it with both hands. It is her mother's scarf, soaked and frayed. When she wakes, it is in the grey pre-dawn light. She lies there, her hands firmly pressed against the cool, dry sheets until the house begins to stir.

June 2011
Niagara Falls, Canada

MY GRANDMOTHER MARKS THE END OF this story by transferring the meat from the skillet to a roasting pan, and I am struck by something vaguely technicolour about these tales. It is something I want to ask about, but the moment passes as my grandmother mixes boiling water with bouillon, adds the hot liquid to the cooling meat. She places the lid on the top of the roaster and puts the roaster in the oven. Her movements take on an uncoordinated tilt and I convince her to lie down. She usually wakes at four a.m., lies in bed until six, then putters quietly in the kitchen. By eleven, she is heavy-eyed and rubbing her lower back. I watch her move stiffly up the short flight of stairs between the basement and the rec room.

I put the butter in the downstairs fridge and collect the few dishes and utensils, balancing the Shake 'n Bake—encrusted spatula on a plate with a fork and knife, and carry the dishes upstairs. From the rec room, I can smell oregano and canned tomatoes and realize my mother has gone ahead with her lasagna. As I turn the corner into the upstairs kitchen, I can hear her humming something under her breath, some late-nineties grunge anthem. Standing at the sink, she looks like a rock'n'roll Sophia Loren, elegant and cool at once, scrubbing tomato residue from a skillet. I am careful to make some noise, rattling a spoon against the plate so as not to startle her when her back is turned. For all her coolness and ready laugh, my mother has my grandmother's tendency to startle, a wariness as deep in the bones as all that love and fierceness.

Though they approach it differently, my mother and grandmother also share their talent for cooking. When I was a child, dinner parties on the island were South Indian feasts of tandoori chicken, cream and cashew corn, prawn curry, and turmeric rice with raisins and toasted almonds — or a Greek night with moussaka and salads laden with feta and firm-fleshed Kalamata olives and silver pans of spanakopita my mother had made that morning following a glossy insert in *Canadian Living*. My mother would roll out phyllo pastry on a wooden board, the same honey colour as the house walls, encouraging me to flour the rolling pin with great childish handfuls that would float in the air like mist.

My parents' dinner crowd was largely made up of neighbours and friends who worked with my parents at the college across the water, many of whom had taught in Beijing or Buenos Aires or Bangkok when this was still an unusual thing to do. Dinner was woven into an electric flow of personal mythology, local gossip, jokes, and political debate. My mother would bring out dishes from the kitchen while my father poured wine for the guests with one hand, gesturing his way through a story with the other. And when they talked about the world, this group recognized themselves in it: my father took some college exchange students to Grenada one year, my mother and I swam at the nutmeg-scented beach where the bombs later fell. When CBC Radio reported a group of Canadian teachers had been in a car crash in China, my parents' crowd immediately knew one of their colleagues was in the car. And that sense that they were about the world and the world was about them charged their political discussions, made them personal, put them at the centre of the universe through some dynamic law.

After dinner and the long, thin Ovations the kids pretended to smoke like mint-chocolate cigarettes, the Scandinavian furniture would be pushed aside and there was dancing, the men twirling in their jeans, dress shirts, and leather vests, the women in their silk blouses over tanned arms and gold chains, the children thrown up in the air, shrieking that the adults should never stop, never stop as Paul Simon sang of days of miracle and wonder and the floorboards shook in that midnight clearing.

My mother was always at the centre of these parties, igniting them with confidence and flair, a moxie I do not naturally possess but will sometimes slip on like a borrowed dress. She was always at the centre of the dancing after dinner, surrounded by the same children who had clamoured around our air mattress at the beach that afternoon. The children would scream, "There's San Miguel! There's Chiang Mai!" They were their parents' children and inheritors of that internal geography even if they themselves had never left the island. My mother would pilot this magic carpet, waist high in blue-green waters, propelling us over seagrass and sand dollars and vast, unvisited countries, as the sun beat down on that sheltered bay.

"Some more dishes for you," I say quietly. My mother gestures with her head toward the empty counter beside the sink. I adjust myself to the altered atmosphere that surrounds her in this house. Here, she is different, pulled closer to the events and mannerisms of her childhood. Sometimes she is louder, she and my grandmother yelling a stream of Russian-Ukrainian that rushes by at a pace far beyond my ability to keep up.

"Why are you arguing?" I ask, distressed by the rising pitch and guttural consonants.

They look at me, surprised. "We not arguing, Sasha," my grandmother says. "We talking about what kind vegetables we put in soup."

But sometimes, as now, my mother is quieter, pulled by a tide I cannot see.

September 1959
Niagara Falls, Canada

LUCY WATCHES THE CRACKS IN THE sidewalk as she walks down the street with Mama. N-I-K-I-F-O-R-T-C-H-U-K. Step. N-I-K-I-F-O-R-T-C-H-U-K. She chants the spelling of her last name, thinking if she can spell it fast enough, her principal will finally figure out it is all one word, and stop calling her Niki — Niki Fortchuk. "No running in the halls, Miss Fortchuk." Dork.

Lucy is glad they are walking to the store instead of driving. Unlike a lot of the other mothers, Mama knows how to drive, which is neat. Mama takes Mrs. Korban shopping sometimes because Mrs. Korban doesn't know how to drive or read English, which is less neat. Mrs. Korban smells like mothballs and always looks sad, always staring, never blinking. But Mama says Lucy should be nice because Mrs. Korban helped them when they first came to Canada. She says this in the same way she says Lucy should be careful not to scratch the paint on the walls with her pogo stick because both she and Pop had to work hard to buy the house. In the beginning, Mama says, there were two other families renting rooms to help pay the mortgage. Lucy doesn't remember this, nor does she know how all these people used to fit in her house.

The September sun is peeking through the dark brown curls of Mama's home permanent. Mama looks nice today, in her yellow dress with brown trim. Lucy pulls on Mama's hand and Mama looks down and smiles at her, fleetingly, before she goes back to list-making inside her head.

As they near the Suburban Store, Lucy can see all of the things for sale behind the glass: lawn furniture and white towels and blue-rimmed dishes and a little ceramic dog. Mama opens the door and a little bell rings at the top and a saleswoman with thick red hair looks up from behind the counter. Mama walks them over to the woman, her sense of mission clear in her steps. Lucy holds her breath for a moment, hoping Mama's accent won't be too thick, that this woman will understand what they need.

"Hello," Mama says carefully. "We would like to buy some elbow grease, please."

The woman looks surprised. Her eyebrows shoot up into her bangs.

"I'm sorry, you —"

"My daughter teacher say she need elbow grease . . . for school. You sell here?"

The woman laughs, but not in a mean way. She has a nice laugh, like Mrs. Buck, Lucy's third-grade teacher.

"Oh," she says. From the way she is talking, slowly and clearly, Lucy can tell she knows Mama doesn't speak English very well. "Elbow grease is an expression. To use elbow grease means to work harder. Your daughter's teacher is saying your daughter could work a little harder in school."

Mama turns to look at Lucy with a sharp movement of her head. Lucy smiles up at Mama and shrugs. Lucy knows she will hear a lot about working harder at school, but for now Mama looks like she's trying not to laugh, too. Mama thanks the saleswoman and they walk out of the store into the early fall sunlight. Lucy knows that Pop and Alex are waiting for them at home. She says the words "elbow grease" to herself, knowing the story will make everyone laugh.

The next day is Saturday and Mama makes fried chicken and potato salad and puts it carefully in the fridge. Then she packs a cooler full of sandwiches and Pop's work thermos full of iced tea. Finally, Mama adds a small jar of her homemade hot pickled peppers, and Lucy eyes them happily. The peppers are her party trick. When Alex has friends over he opens up a jar, slices small pieces of the oozing pepper, shiny in chili oil, and hands out little pieces to his friends. They all make gagging noises, overdoing it the way boys do, fanning their tongues. Then Alex will say, "Watch this!" and Lucy will take a whole pepper from the jar and eat it slowly, casually, the hot oil dripping off the stem. The pepper burns her tongue, but it isn't unpleasant. It's worth it to see the boys gasp. She likes it when Alex says: "See, my little sister can eat a whole one, you sissies."

Pop packs up the Chevrolet with towels and a beach blanket. Alex brings some comic books — *Captain America* and *Captain Marvel* — and jumps in the back beside Lucy, swatting her for no reason. Mama sits in the front beside Pop, the lunch cooler at her feet. They'll drop Mama off at work and go to the beach all day, then Pop will drive back into town and pick her up when her shift is over, stopping to get the chicken dinner out of the fridge on the way back. When Pop works at the factory, it's the other way around, but at the end of a beach day, they always have dinner all together on a blanket in the sand.

Pop drives the car through town and they drop Mama off on the sidewalk outside the Jade Garden. She blows them a kiss as she gets out. "Be careful, okay?" she says, in her worried way, like she thinks something will go wrong, something terrible, while they are out of sight. Lucy waves until her mother walks through the glass door of the restaurant. Pop drives on to the beach, singing "Che Sera." He hums the words he doesn't know and Lucy joins in on "whatever will be." Alex thinks he is too old to sing and reads his comics. The air from the cool September morning pours through the open windows. They will be at the beach all day, maybe twelve hours, and Lucy hopes they will be the first car in the parking lot.

They are, in fact, the first to arrive at Sherkston Beach. Pop pulls up into a spot facing the water and Alex and Lucy help him lug the towels and beach blanket and lunch to a spot on the sand. When they have arranged their things, Alex throws a towel on his head like Lawrence of Arabia.

"No prisoners!" he yells to the empty beach, thrusting his arms into the air, "No prisoners!" He runs up the side of the sand dune with a crazy shriek.

Lucy starts running too and she can hear Pop behind her, laughing. The sand is still cool on her bare feet but it will get hotter as the day goes on until the soles of her feet get red and crispy and some of the skin peels away.

When the sun is high they swim in the lake, and by late afternoon Lucy's eyes are burning from the glare. People are all around, most of them swimming or wading in small groups by the shore. A man comes along selling ice cream but they have lots of food. Teenagers are hanging out in the parking lot, listening to some song called "Wad I Say" on the radio.

"Hey-Hey-Hey-Hey," Lucy sings along, digging in the sand with her heels. She looks over at Alex, who is reading his comic book on the blanket beside her.

"What's a wad?"

"What?"

"What's a wad? Like 'Wad I say'?"

Alex rolls his eyes. "You're a wad, dork face."

Lucy punches his shoulder harder than she knows she should and is rewarded with a loud "ow."

Alex balls his fist to retaliate but Lucy says, "Pop's coming," then scans the lake to see if this true.

In the distance, she sees her father swimming toward her, pushing his body through the water with strong, smooth strokes. He makes the other swimmers look like they aren't moving at all. When he gets out he grabs one of the blue towels Mama ironed yesterday. His body makes a shadow standing over them, and Lucy puts a hand to her forehead so that she can see his face.

"I'm going to pick up your mother," he says in Russian. "Be careful and don't go in past your armpits." He makes a sideways gesture with his hand, slapping the side of his muscled chest where it meets his arm. He gives Lucy a kiss on the cheek. "Don't let the fairies steal you."

Lucy grins, then asks: "What's a wad, Pop?"

"What you talking 'bout, Lucy?"

Lucy pauses. The last time she asked Pop what something meant she repeated words she had heard in the grocery store, when a man called them "dirty commies." Remembering the look on his face, she shakes her head in a never-mind gesture. The faster he goes the faster he will come back. Alex is still reading comics, so Lucy gets up to collect pebbles on the shore. She wanders the shore, looking at the teenage girls in their bikinis, the scent of hotdogs in the air. A group of boys Alex's age run past her into water, splashing her, but it doesn't matter. It's hot and the spray feels good. She sees a pink stone and picks it up, turning it over. It's a nice one, rose-coloured with white stripes, and she holds it tightly in her hand as she walks along the packed, wet sand.

When Pop gets back with Mama, the parking lot is busy and they have to park far away. Mama looks overheated and gets in the water right away, holding her head above the water line so that her hair won't get wet. Lucy swims beside her and Alex and Pop do underwater handstands. When everyone has cooled down, they sit and eat Mama's fried chicken and potato salad, the heavy sun now low in the sky. After dinner, they pack up and shake the sand out of the blanket, returning to the Chevrolet with their beach things. When they are back on the highway, Pop stretches his arm across the back of the front seat. "Good night, Irene, good night, Irene, I see you in my dreams," he sings. Mama smiles. She is always more relaxed on car rides, where there is nothing for her to do.

Sergei, Irina, and Lucy,
Sherkston Beach, 1959

When they get home, Pop pulls the Chevrolet into the driveway. Mama unlocks the house and Alex and Lucy unload the beach gear and dirty plates. On her second trip back to the car, Lucy notices Pop staring across the road. Two men are standing at the bus stop, smoking. Both wear light beige trench coats. Lucy thinks they must be hot on this warm evening.

"Anything else, Pop?" Lucy asks.

"Go in the house." Pop's voice is hard and Lucy is startled.

Pop puts a hand on her sore shoulder, steering her toward the door. He leaves the Chevrolet trunk open. When they get inside, Pop locks the door and walks swiftly through the house to the kitchen. Lucy follows and finds her mother filling the sink with hot water. Pop says something to Mama in a low voice and they both look across the street to the bus stop. Lucy feels sweat forming at the back of her neck and her stomach muscles feel tight. She can hear Alex turn the television on in the background, blaring the cheery tones of a chewing gum commercial.

"Mama," she says. "I have a sunburn."

"Okay, Lucy. Okay." Mama takes Lucy's hand and leads her into the green-tiled bathroom. The wallpaper has sailboats on it, little ships riding the waves. Pop picked it because he says it reminds him that he was once a sailor. Lucy stands with her arms on the cool white counter as Mama applies the Noxzema to her shoulders. Mama seems distracted, not as gentle as usual, and her fingers are hard and full of tension.

The next morning the strange men are still there, standing at the bus stop. Pop paces in front of the window, still wearing yesterday's clothes. There is stubble on his chin and his eye are glassy. An ashtray on the table is overflowing, an empty package of Export As beside it. Lucy decides to figure out what's wrong and moves to take his hand, but Alex holds her by the elbow.

"Not now," he says in a grown-up voice. Lucy pulls her arm back and marches down the stairs to the basement, looking for Mama. She finds her ironing their clothes for church. She had almost forgotten it was Sunday.

Mama looks up and gives her a distracted smile before going back to working out a crease in Pop's brown church pants.

"What's wrong with Pop?" Lucy asks. She hopes her father won't stay like this for long. He is like a stranger.

Her mother sighs and looks up. Lucy straightens her shoulders and does her best to look mature.

"Tell me," she says.

Mama shrugs and Lucy thinks she is going to tell. When there is danger, Mama always tells. But this time a strange look comes over her face, which is already taut with worry. Before Lucy can ask more questions, Mama pushes her yellow dress at her. The collar is starched and Lucy knows it will be itchy and uncomfortable.

"Go put on dress, Lucy. We late for church."

In the car, Pop deliberately drives away from the men, taking the long way around Dunn Street, the cords in his neck visible and his shoulders locked. At church, Mama buys more votive candles than usual. She crosses herself and guides Lucy into a pew. Alex sits with some of his friends across the way. Mama gives him a warning look. Pop stays outside smoking during the service. Lucy wonders if Mama and Pop will argue about this later.

Church seems to go on forever. Normally Mama likes to stand around with the other women after the service, but today she hurries to the doors. Pop is waiting outside. When he sees them he drops his cigarette and stamps it out. Wordlessly, they cross the parking lot and get in the car. At home, the men in trench coats are still standing by the bus stop. The men stay there for three days, smoking. Buses stop for them but they never get on. Pop watches them, his face patterned by the lace shadows of the living room curtains. On the fourth day, the men disappear.

June 2011
Niagara Falls, Canada

MY MOTHER FINISHES THIS STRANGE TALE, places the colander in the drying rack. It is not that I haven't heard this story before, but it is always a puzzle.

"And you didn't ever find out who the men were?" I ask.

"No. They were there for a few days, then left."

"And Baba and Didi never explained?"

My mother shakes her head.

"Trench coats?"

"It was the fifties. That's what men wore."

I consider this for a moment, then shake my head, doubtfully.

My mother looks at me. Her eyes are dark brown, like my grandmother's, and unlike mine, which are green and getting lighter every year, as though bleached by the sun. She gives me a classic and self-consciously Slavic "What are you going to do?" shrug. It is the shrug of failed crops and political deceit and recognition of life's inherent lack of fairness or reward or basic logic. Here in the kitchen, with spice jars lined neatly on the top of the stove, it makes me smile.

"Wake up Baba," she says. "I'll get lunch going."

I climb the stairs and make my way down the hall to my grandmother's room. The door is half open and I can see her lying on the bedspread, eyes closed, the lacy pattern of the curtain playing shadow games on her white blouse. There is fatigue in her face, some purple smudging around the skin under her eyes and the lines around her mouth are deeper. I hesitate.

"I no sleeping, Sasha," she says. "Come in."

I take a small step into the bedroom. Then hover a moment in front of the dresser.

"Do you want to sleep, Baba? You could have lunch later."

"No, no. I not sleeping. Just rest little bit."

She elbows herself up against the eyelet pillowcases behind her.

"Come in, Sasha," she says again. "Bring me that blue box on dresser. One with gold trim."

I scan the assorted cosmetic bottles that are neatly lined up on a gold-rimmed decorative tray with a mirrored bottom. To the right is a small blue cardboard box, which I carry over to my grandmother. She grasps the box and pats the mattress beside her. I sit as she opens it. Inside, there are three small bottles of perfume nestled in dark blue plastic cutouts.

"Someone give me these perfumes for Christmas," she says. "Smell nice. Maybe you take one, wear to party sometime. "

Her fingers scramble against the cardboard as she pulls out one of the vials. With difficulty, she pulls off the black plastic cap and the air is filled with the scent of wild roses and musk. She cocks her head to the side, considers the scent, then replaces the cap and presses the small smooth bottle into my hand.

"Here, you take."

"No, Baba, it's yours.

"You take, Sasha. It's yours."

"Oh really? What about this bedspread? It's nice."

"Yes, take. You take it."

"And these pillows you embroidered?"

"Yes, take them. Take. Take."

"How about the bed and dresser set. You think it would fit on the plane?"

"Okay, okay. You think you smart. But perfume, I want you to have." She looks toward the windows. "Someone give me perfume once. Was long time ago, during war."

I try to think of a joke, an anecdote, anything to break the rhythm of surfacing and immersion, surfacing and immersion that has suffused this morning. But it is the rhythm of this house, and I know I stand little chance.

"I keep that bottle all through war. When things bad, I smell it and it smells like better time, you understand? Like I could smell better time before it happen."

My grandmother's eyes wander back to my face, seeing me but failing to take in my reluctance to be dragged into all of this, this long-ago time that has so little to do with now. I return her gaze with intensity, throwing out a line, willing her back.

"I keep that bottle all through war and long time after."

December 1942
Wet{lar, Germany

IRINA IS FLOATING. SHE HEARS CHILDREN singing. The boys' choir?
There are definitely children's voices, but mixed with giggles, and
adult voices too, high-spirited and off-key. There is a knock at the
door and then Frau Elsie's voice calling out.

"Irina, are you dressed? We're on our way in."

Irina pulls the covers over the ribbons that lace the front of her
nightgown. The door opens. Frau Elsie is carrying one of Frau
Lichen's vanilla cakes. The children and the staff surround her as
they finish their birthday song. Irina participated in the same ritual
for Friedrich's birthday in October, but she thought it was only for
the long-time staff. The singers hold on to the last note and it wavers
against the walls of the small room, filling it with discordant, happy
noise. Everyone claps, Karin the longest and the hardest, her face
bright with excitement.

"Take this to the kitchen, will you, Heidi?" Frau Elsie asks, handing the cake over. "Breakfast cake for everyone this morning!"

The children and staff follow Heidi to the kitchen, laughing and chatting. Frau Elsie approaches Irina's bed, her face mischievous with surprise. Tucked under her arm she has a flat, rectangular package wrapped in brown paper with a yellow ribbon. She sits down at the end of Irina's bed and hands it to her.

"Open it."

Irina handles the package carefully and pulls gently on the ribbon to open the present. Inside are a white wool sweater, a light blue silk scarf, and a small black leather purse. Irina feels something square inside the purse and opens the zipper. She pulls out the little bottle of amber liquid and looks up at Elsie, overwhelmed.

"Don't even think about crying, Irina! It's only a few small things. Now get dressed and come to the kitchen for some cake. I want you to come out with me this morning."

Irina dresses quickly and brings the perfume bottle to her nose but decides to save it for special occasions. She places it back in the purse, and the purse on top of the sweater on the wardrobe shelf. She ties the scarf around her neck, enjoying the feeling of it against her skin. When she reaches the kitchen, everyone is in a good mood, not just because it is Irina's birthday but also because it is almost Christmas Eve. Knut speaks with Friedrich about the best way to cut down the Christmas tree. Friedrich nods gravely. Frau Vogel and Frau Lichen discuss the Christmas menu. Heidi hands Irina a piece of cake on a blue-rimmed china plate.

"Happy Birthday!" she says. "How much better you look than when you first came. You almost fill out that dress, now. You'll end up with a boyfriend yet!" She steps closer to Irina. "Do you know it's Frau Elsie's birthday today, too? The family will have a party for her later but she said the morning should be yours."

Irina ducks her head with embarrassment and sits at the far end of the table. Leah and Marina come over to chat with her. By seven-thirty it is time to get to work and the kitchen empties of people and sound.

Frau Elsie, who disappeared early, returns to the kitchen dressed in her camel coat and black gloves.

"Meet me outside, Irina," she says, her manner less playful than earlier. "Friedrich is loading the car."

Irina returns to her room for the grey wool coat Frau Elsie gave her for the winter season and hurries out to the garage. Friedrich is stacking boxes and bags into the trunk of the car. Frau Elsie opens the door to the backseat herself and motions to Irina to join her.

"We are going to the camp, Irina," Frau Elsie, says. "I don't want you to be afraid. We have papers for you and there is no way they can keep you there."

Irina freezes. The idea of returning terrifies her, but she manages to force herself into the car. Friedrich slides into the driver's seat and rubs his gloved hands together against the cold. He glances in the rearview mirror and Frau Elsie nods.

Irina has difficulty interpreting Frau Elsie's mood and decides it is better to stay quiet. She fingers the new scarf at her throat. Halfway down the hill, Frau Elsie shrugs.

"How old are you then, Irina?"

"Twenty."

"Twenty," Frau Elsie repeats a little distantly. "I was in school when I was twenty."

Heidi told Irina that Frau Elsie herself is thirty-nine today, though her employer seems not so much celebratory as abstracted. In the quiet, Irina listens to the smooth hum of the engine as they make their way down the hill.

"Things were very bad after the first war," Frau Elsie says, suddenly turning her body toward Irina as though she has come to some decision. "We were fortunate, of course, with the factory. Father had food brought in for the employees. But for most, bread cost double and then ten, then fifty times what it used to."

Frau Elsie pauses for a moment, searching for the right words.

"People couldn't feed their families. And there came this point — this point where bread was no longer bread, but a lever."

This is the closest Frau Elsie has come to broaching the circumstances of the war. Irina knows calling Hitler's aggression anything other than a glorious campaign is punishable, that even this vague allusion to the rage and despair that brought him to power is a risk. This risk hangs in the air between the women and Irina senses it is a kind of collusion Frau Elsie has created between them ahead of their arrival at the camp. Irina nods, hoping Frau Elsie will see she understands — and she does, well accustomed to the sideways referencing of basic facts suppressed by authorities. It was a mode of communication she had become aware of as a child of collectivization and had mastered as a college student in the communist system. Frau Elsie watches her carefully for a moment then returns the nod. In the silence that follows, both women look out at the snow-rimmed roof of the medieval cathedral.

When they reach the guard post, Friedrich presents papers to the soldier on duty. The guard inspects the papers, looks in the back at the two women, and waves them through. Friedrich drives to the women's barracks. As she climbs out of the car, Irina is overwhelmed by the familiar stench of turnip that comes from the nearby kitchen as Friedrich unloads the boxes and bags onto the frozen ground.

As Irina and Frau Elsie wait, a young Gestapo officer and his secretary round the corner. The officer is performing an inspection and is dictating notes. The officer pauses when he sees Frau Elsie. Irina wills herself into invisibility, and indeed it seems to work, for he pretends not to see her at all.

"Frau Kühn-Leitz," the officer says.

"Inspector Mauer," Frau Elsie says, equally cool.

The officer is tall, with dark hair and blue eyes and extremely white teeth. It is the Gestapo that polices the camp, that administers punishment, that roots out information, that brings dogs in the night. Knowing what she knows, Irina cannot fathom how this man can look so clean. Mauer eyes the boxes on the ground.

"I have urged you before, Frau Kühn-Leitz, not to bring things into the camp."

"My role here is authorized," Frau Elsie says calmly.

"All the more reason. It is unwise, very unwise, to treat subhumans too humanely. It confuses the issue."

Frau Elsie says nothing but neither does she break eye contact. There is a moment where Irina thinks Mauer is going to press, but he nods once and continues on, the secretary giving the car and boxes a final glance as he walks toward the guardhouse.

Frau Elsie is still for a moment, looking over the fence and up the hill toward Haus Friedwart. Then she straightens her shoulders and turns toward Irina. "Take those bags, please, Irina. Friedrich and I should be able to manage the boxes."

Arms full of packages, the three of them approach the barrack door. This is not Irina's dormitory, though the squat construction and metal roof are the same. Irina hears children's voices, a cry. Peering over the top of the boxes in his arms, Friedrich opens the door and lets it close behind them.

Inside, small children are everywhere, possibly fifteen of them, a mayhem of unsupervised activity. A gang of small boys jumps on beds in a corner. A skinny toddler, dressed in droopy rags, runs past them, reeking of urine and feces. At the far end of the room, babies in dresser drawers and cardboard boxes wail, older cries mixed in with the bleating urgency of newborns. One of the older girls, aged five or six, dashes back and forth from one to the other, trying desperately to quiet them. Some children lie in their beds, staring at nothing. Some have heads shorn for lice, bony faces and wide eyes. From her time in the camp, Irina knows that the children stay behind while their mothers are sent to work in the factory.

When the children see Frau Elsie, many of them run over to her and pull at her skirt.

"Lady, you've come back! Please, something to eat?" a little boy with darting brown eyes asks in halting German, and it turns into a kind of chant among the children.

"You will eat," Frau Elsie yells above the clamour, using gestures to make herself understood. "But first you must be quiet. Everyone sit on that side of the room."

Frau Elsie points to the least cluttered wall, and the children run over and sit, some bouncing up and down on their heels.

"Irina," Frau Elsie says, "start handing out sandwiches from that box. Friedrich will pass out the milk."

Irina takes a box and begins at one end of the row, handing egg and ham sandwiches into small fingers. Some of the children eat like hungry animals, while others eat slowly, in dull, mechanical bites. When Irina looks up, Friedrich is pouring milk into bowls, which are passed down the line.

At the far end of the room, Frau Elsie is changing a baby, replacing soiled rags with a cloth diaper. Once the children are fed, they begin moving around the room again. The frenzied edge of hunger blunted, their games are less frenetic. Once she has retrieved the milk bowls from the last child, Irina joins Frau Elsie and helps with the babies. There is nothing new for her in babies being left most of the day. In Stanytsia babies were swaddled so tightly in rags that they stood upright against the wall while the women worked in the fields. But even under the strict labour rules of the Collective, at least one woman was left behind to watch over them.

Once the babies are changed, Frau Elsie fills bottles with milk and feeds two at a time, one with each hand, two little forms on either side of her on an unmade cot. Irina follows her lead. One of her babies sucks hungrily from the bottle. The other can barely move his lips, much of the milk dribbling out. His eyes are closed and he has dark pouches in the skin beneath. Irina looks up at the older children who are playing a game of hide and seek with Friedrich at the other end of the room. By design, there are few places to hide: under the single beds or under the few clothes that hang on the hooks that line the walls. But Friedrich pretends not to see the children as he walks by them, loudly asking where they could be, then roars as he feigns the discovery of a little boy with bristles of red hair growing in across his scalp. Friedrich tickles the boy as he lifts him in the air.

Before leaving, Friedrich, Irina and Frau Elsie hand out dolls and wooden toys from the final boxes. A girl with wispy brown pigtails clutches a doll to her chest. The boys play war games with the wooden planes. The girl turns to Frau Elsie and asks her a question in Ukrainian.

"What is she saying?" Frau Elsie asks Irina.

"She asks if you are a queen, and if you will take her with you to your castle," Irina translates, holding her voice steady.

The little girl's eyes shine with expectation, and she stands on her toes.

Frau Elsie bites her lip for a moment then crouches down so that she is eye to eye with the girl.

"Tell her," she says to Irina, though she speaks directly to the girl in a low, confiding voice. "Right now there are dragons around my castle, but I hope one day it will be safe for her to come visit me."

Irina translates. The girl's lips twist in disappointment, but she seems satisfied with the logic of this explanation.

Friedrich gathers the boxes while Frau Elsie knocks on the door. The guard opens it to let the three adults out and closes the door behind them. The voices of the children fade as they walk down the hallway. In the car, Irina again holds her breath as they pull up to the guard post, but after some cursory words, they leave the camp.

Irina thinks of her youngest brother, Misha, the way he held onto her leg the day she was taken from her village.

"Thank you."

Frau Elsie's face looks dark in the afternoon light. Her mood has changed and when they come, her words are terse. "I am German. Their mothers are working in our factory. What small acts can excuse that?"

When they return to the house, Frau Elsie walks swiftly indoors. Irina helps Friedrich unload. Friedrich has been silent since leaving the camp, his playful demeanour with the children retreating into something much older. The question that has been rocking around inside Irina's head suddenly comes out in the cool air of the garage.

"Why do they let her?"

Friedrich considers this for a moment, then shrugs, stuffing his hands into the pockets of his coat.

"She's a Leitz. The Nazis need the Leitzes."

"But aren't we — enemy people?"

Friedrich sniffs at this phrase, then turns to stacking boxes against the wall of the garage. Irina continues to stare.

"She's been given a long leash," Friedrich says at last, the final box stacked neatly inside the rest. "No one knows how far it stretches, probably not even her."

Irina stands there for a moment, feeling the cold cement of the garage floor through the soles of her boots. When Friedrich says nothing more, she walks out of the garage into the winter air, her hands in the pockets of her coat. The sky has darkened, and as Irina crosses the yard, she feels a snowflake land on her cheek. On the first floor, the light is on in Herr Leitz's room. Irina can see him standing at the window, his face obscured, looking out over the expanse of frozen grass.

June 2011
Niagara Falls, Canada

IN THE LATE AFTERNOON, MY GRANDMOTHER lies on the living room couch, a cream crocheted blanket covering her legs. My mother, legs tucked under, sits on the La-Z-Boy recliner. I lie on the carpet, feeling the carpet fibres under my fingertips. There is a soap opera on television, a show my grandmother has watched for over thirty years. The characters have seen her through her own troubles and when she speaks of them, it is with a sense of kinship, as though they are long-lost relatives from Kyiv.

I am aware of the television voices, but inwardly I piece together a puzzle of second-hand memories and fragments gleaned online after lunch. The central, surprising revelation is Ernst Leitz II's status as a less well-known Schindler. Before the war closed Germany's borders, Leitz made sustained efforts to smuggle his Jewish employees and other at-risk members of Wetzlar's photographic community out of Germany. Officially, Ernst Leitz rescued forty-one people from persecution by sending them to foreign branches of the Leica company. Some were

Leitz employees and members of their families. Other German Jews were offered "apprenticeships" that saw them transferred to Leica offices in New York, London, Singapore, or Hong Kong. Leitz is further acknowledged to have helped twenty-three people circumvent Nazi laws against marriages between Jewish and non-Jewish Germans. The real numbers are likely much higher. One of the New York Leica employees, a twenty-five-year-old ad man at the time named Norman Lipton, recalls that in the period between 1938 and 1940, twenty to thirty exhausted men and women, all German-Jewish refugees, would appear every few weeks in the New York office with luggage and Leica cameras around their necks. Leica executives would scramble to find work for the new arrivals, either with Leica or companies like Kodak or Ilex. Other reports suggest Leitz would pay these recent immigrants three months' salary until they were on their feet.

Elsie Kühn-Leitz helped her father in this enterprise despite the risks: Edwin Türk, Leica's sales director in Wetzlar, was jailed by the Gestapo for writing a recommendation letter enabling the U.S. emigration of a Jewish family called Ehrenfeld at Leitz's behest. The letter was intercepted and the family's two sons were imprisoned at Buchenwald in 1938. As the visa was already in process, however, the sons were miraculously released and the family was able to emigrate via London to the United States. Ernst Leitz provided them with enough Leica photographic equipment to start a business in Florida. When Türk was arrested in January of 1939 for his role in the escape, Leitz travelled to Berlin and negotiated a substantial bribe. Türk was released on the condition Leitz fire him immediately. Leitz agreed, though secretly continued to pay Türk's salary throughout the war.

While Ernst Leitz's smuggling efforts were later dubbed "The Leica Freedom Train," Leitz himself refused to speak of this time, never told his grandchildren, forbade one of his sons from speaking to the press when questions were asked in the sixties, insisting it was only what any decent person in his position would have done. Many of these stories were later uncovered and documented by a California rabbi named Frank Dabba Smith. Leitz's documented resistance activities seem to have mostly taken place pre-war. But my grandmother's account of war-time visitors to the house makes me wonder how much she saw, how much she knew, even as I question the good of confronting her with information beyond what she herself has told us.

On the TV screen, a wealthy heiress has been abducted by her long-lost twin and her gang of unsavoury friends.

"This rerun," my grandmother says, sensing my eyes on her. "Classic episode because long weekend coming. Catherine 'popravilisa,' you can see in her face. Kidnappers feed her too many potato chip. See pizza box everywhere?"

Literally, popravilisa means to "right oneself," which means to gain weight. My grandmother has come to realize that comments about those of us who have "righted" ourselves are poorly received by the family, and now mostly confines these observations to television characters. Maybe because it is a rerun, but more likely because of the importance of the weekend ahead, my grandmother is only half watching, her mouth moving in her silent act of list-making.

"Tomorrow we make vareniki," my grandmother says. Her jaw is set and I glance over at my mother. I watch my mother consider the argument, trace it through to its inevitable conclusion, then let it go. My grandmother nods.

"Also grocery shopping. Cherry on sale at Zehrs. Good price. And No Frills. Maybe Walmarts."

My mother stays quiet. This careful choosing of battles is new, a response to what she has observed over the five days we have been here — my grandmother's occasionally unsteady balance and previously unthinkable inability to summon up a date or a name. Even last year this might have been a battle royale, my mother insisting my grandmother not tire herself with all this shopping, my grandmother arguing that she doesn't sleep anyway, so what's the difference? My grandmother listens for the break in my mother's silence. Not hearing one, she counts up her victories.

"We eleven people Saturday, Lucy?" my grandmother asks. "Everyone?"

"Everyone," my mother confirms and counts the family on her fingers: the three of us; my uncle Alex; his wife, Debi, Alex's three grown children, my cousins Tara, Laura, and Deidre; and Tara's daughter, Madison. But with the last two fingers my mother also counts Laurie and Jerry Johnson, because Laurie's family and ours forged a bond in a displaced persons camp in Germany in 1946 that has survived time and immigration: my grandparents to Niagara Falls and Laurie's family, Milka and Panas Kantowsky and their two girls, Laura and Valya, to Rochester, New York. When ten years later Laura, turned Laurie, met and married Jerry, tall and blue-eyed with faultless manners, they soon moved into an airy rancher on a cul-de-sac in the grassy suburb of Pittsford. It was, through the eyes of the older women, the realization of the dream they had clung to across oceans, the better life my grandmother had smelled in a perfume bottle, now made visible in the young couple's spacious kitchen, in Laurie's pretty cocktail dresses, Jerry's business lunches and summer weekends at the cottage.

My grandmother sighs. "Too bad we no have time to go over the river, maybe buy some big tubs ice cream."

"Up for a bit of smuggling, Baba?"

It is well-known in the family what my grandmother does with the modest forced labour reparation cheques she receives in U.S. dollars from Germany. She buys dairy products in bulk at a substantially reduced price from the giant supermarkets on the American side of the Falls. She then hides these items under a brown blanket in her trunk to avoid paying duty, plying an addled old lady act for the border guards.

"That not smuggling, Sasha," my grandmother says. "Little bit grocery like that don't make no difference to no one."

"Border town skills," my mother agrees. "In high school, my friends and I used to go shopping over the bridge in one outfit and wear five home, one on top of the other."

"What would the border guards say?"

"They asked if we had a big lunch."

My grandmother laughs at this, revelling in the lawlessness of it all. She wears the same look on her face when she guns the Oldsmobile down the highway after a successful smuggling run. She is still chuckling as a shower gel commercial ends. The soap opera returns, and a groomed couple appear in a substantial living room with powder-blue walls and mahogany bookshelves. They are arguing, as though they have absorbed, through the screen, the argument that has failed to take place in this living room. I tune out their voices, still drifting along in the other plotline with the unknown twin, maybe because it reminds me of a story my father once told me.

This was 1969, when my father was in his mid-twenties and Torremolinos, on Spain's Costa del Sol, was still closer to the fishing village it once was than the mega-resort it would become. Still half under the shadow of Franco, the low-rise stucco buildings that lined the main drag leading to the beach were scuffed and shuttered. The Mediterranean sun was high and shone down on signs for tobaco and cerveza. Only two men were out: my father and the man walking toward him. At first my father took the man for just another tourist heading back from the beach to his hostel or van. But as the men neared, each was stopped by the shock of recognition. The stranger was an inch or two taller, but the men were otherwise identical: same dark curling hair, same eyes the colour of curaçao, same beard over high cheekbones leading to prominent ears, same bookish intensity that showed itself in the assessing look and full, pursed lips. Graspingly, the men traded information with the little language they had in common: my father's name, Brian, the fact that he lived in Toronto. The man was French-Canadian. His name was Philippe. Still staring at their reflections but unable to get any further in their exchange, the men shook hands and went their separate ways. Deeply affected in the moment, the incident faded from my father's mind until many months later, a young woman ran up to my father in a Vancouver pub, crying "Philippe! Philippe!"

"No," my father said. "But I know who you mean."

I have often wondered about this, about the double who may be out there. I look like my mother, same long neck, almond eyes, and forthright nose, but because of the age difference and our different colouring, we are only mistaken for each other on the phone. My uncle Alex is often taken for Barry Manilow, and fans are offended when he won't sign autographs or sing a line from "Copacabana," but this desire for a brush with celebrity is not quite what I mean. I mean the everyday double who is wandering around somewhere, the chance encounter in a coffee shop or outside a bookstore or in line at the bank.

"I no like that Adrian," my grandmother says suddenly. She speaks with such force that it takes me a moment to realize she is talking about one of the soap opera characters. "He not nice to Cassandra. Remind me Elsie husband."

December 1942
Wetzlar, Germany

THE DAY BEFORE CHRISTMAS, FRIEDRICH INSTALLS a large pine tree in the main hall. The needles look very green against the cream walls. Irina has never heard of this, bringing a live tree into a house. At home, trees were for firewood. Nonetheless, she enjoys the scent of the pine needles and other festive touches around the house: the dark red velvet bows on the banisters and the wooden soldiers lined up in the children's playroom.

After lunch, Frau Elsie's husband, Herr Kurt, arrives from Munich. He is tall with light hair and wears a German military uniform. He hands Irina his trench coat at the door, nods formally, and walks up the main staircase to Frau Elsie's suite. Indistinctly, Irina hears the children's cries and running feet, followed by a more measured greeting from Frau Elsie.

The following day, the children run around the house, unsure whether to help organize the candles for the tree, search for their presents, or sneak sweets. Knut almost runs into Irina as she brings the good silver up the stairs from where she has been cleaning it on the table in the kitchen. "Sorry!" he yells as he barrels down the stairs.

Irina hears an exclamation from Heidi as something clatters to the floor. Frau Elsie seems at turns joyful and distracted, directing the arrangements for dinner and running after the children. By five o'clock, Friedrich has attached all of the white candles to the tree branches and the family and staff gather around the tree. Friedrich turns off the electric lights and the room is filled with the soft glow of the candles among the pine needles. There is some singing of carols that Irina doesn't know. She imagines her mother gathering supplies for the Christmas basket, which her father will secretly have blessed by the priest two weeks from now, during Christmas on the Eastern Orthodox calendar. She wonders if her family will be able to find fish this year for a special dinner, if they are all still together. Irina looks across the room to where Marina and Leah are standing and wonders if they are thinking the same.

After the lighting of the tree, the family lingers in the music room before making their way to the table, with its red candles and attractive centrepiece. With all the dishes Frau Lichen has prepared, Frau Vogel has determined that both Heidi and Irina will serve. Between the excited chatter of the children and the loud voice of Herr Kurt, who started drinking schnapps early in the afternoon, the house is filled with sound.

As Irina rounds the staircase with a platter of venison, she hears Frau Elsie and Herr Kurt on the landing. She slows a little to allow them time to enter the dining room.

". . . have to wear that to dinner?" Frau Elsie asks in a low voice.

"Your father is . . . uniformed or not. I'm on leave but not immune to being hauled in."

"You know very well Father had to join," Frau Elsie says severely. "What choice did he have?"

"Choice?" Herr Kurt says briskly. "I, at least, was drafted. Not all of us are profiting quite so handsomely from this war. Not all of us —"

Kurt pauses for a moment as Irina appears at the top of the stairs. Irina lowers her eyes as she passes them. Peripherally, she can see that Frau Elsie's face is taut. When she speaks, it is quietly but with a gravelly tension Irina has rarely heard.

"Would you have him arrested or ejected from his own company like — like Junkers? These people are dangerous and they take. They take what they want. What is he supposed to —"

"Yes, yes," Kurt says. "Poor Father. What was he supposed to do?" Kurt turns abruptly from Frau Elsie and follows Irina into the dining room. Herr Leitz sits at the head of the table. Herr Kurt takes the chair at the opposing end. Knut and Karin sit on one side of the table and Frau Elsie, smoothing her skirt, takes the chair on the other side, beside Karin.

"Cornelia," Frau Elsie says, keeping her voice steady, "your father missed the Christmas concert at school. I am sure he would like to hear your song."

Cornelia stands next to the table, clearly trying to help her mother restore some sense of harmony to the evening. She sings a short lullaby about the dark winter forest, her voice high and clear. Everyone claps.

"Very nice, Cornelia, very nice," Kurt says, spearing the venison with a pronged serving fork with a force that makes the platter vibrate in Irina's hands. "So tell me, what else are they teaching you at that school?"

Cornelia and Knut begin talking about their classes, which allows some of the tension to dissipate. By the time Irina returns with a custard cinnamon cake, the table conversation seems to be holding steady.

After dinner, Irina, Frau Lichen, and Frau Vogel attend the evening church service with the family and again Irina is most moved by the singing of the choir, the way the boys' voices fill the church with a pure and youthful intensity. Elsie, too, seems to find her balance in the music, her eyes fixed on Knut's earnest, impish face in the choir's centre row.

As much of the German staff has been given the evening to be with their families, Irina helps put the children to bed. Knut has difficulty calming down after the triumph of his performance and jumps up and down on his mattress until Irina tells him Father Christmas might be watching. Cornelia hums the song she sang at dinner.

"Will it snow tonight, Irina?" she asks.

"I don't know, Cornelia, but it will be Christmas Day just the same."

"Snow makes everything beautiful."

"Yes, it does."

Irina brushes the girl's blonde hair with a wide wooden brush and turns out the light in the bedroom.

"Will you leave the hall light on?" Cornelia asks.

"Yes, of course."

"Is Mama coming to say goodnight?"

"I am sure she will."

On the way downstairs, Irina passes Frau Elsie's rooms. She listens for a moment to see if she is coming to say goodnight to the children. She does not hear anything. With Herr Kurt in the house, everything is slightly off-kilter.

In her own room, Irina sits on her bed without turning on the light. *Herr Leitz is a Nazi*, she thinks mechanically, wrapping her mind around this new information. For a moment, the knowledge sears her. But it is only one side of a complicated equation. In the night, people often come to the house, their faces bright with panic. There is a shuffling in the study, whispered conversations, phone calls, Herr Leitz or Frau Elsie calling for sandwiches to be bundled for travel, the visitors looking grim but resolved by the time they leave, packages in arms. There are the visits to the children's camp. There are the servants, sheltered behind these walls. *These are good people*, Irina thinks fiercely. *They are good.* She holds firmly to this conviction as the snowflakes fall outside her window, blurring the outlines of the garden path.

June 2011
Niagara Falls, Canada

"FRAU ELSIE WAS GOOD WOMAN," my grandmother says with finality. "Like angel she was."

She clears her throat and looks determinedly at her soap opera, where a new group of characters has gathered around a swimming pool for a Fourth of July party that will play out all week. My mother and I exchange glances across the living room. I know we are thinking the same thing — that we have never heard this version, not the details about Kurt Kühn, not the shadow of Ernst Leitz's party membership. It feels like discovering an unexpected room in a familiar house.

This sense stays with me into the long afternoon, and I allow myself to be drawn back online. More targeted searching reveals that Ernst Leitz did indeed join the Nazi Party in 1942, though he had stood as a candidate for the left-leaning German Democratic Party during the Weimar Republic. Leitz's progressive actions are well documented: he was one of the first German employers to initiate a health and welfare plan; he created a grocery-credit program and imported food from Denmark so that his employees could afford to eat during the hyper-inflation of the 1920s; he was instrumental to the "training program" that saw workers in his own company and beyond escape concentration camps. During the postwar reckoning, Ernst Leitz II was not found to have committed any wrongdoing and Leica, along with the German government and over two thousand German companies, paid into a 7.5 billion dollar reparation fund in 1999. Nonetheless, the facts of forced labour and party membership remain.

When the sun is lower, my grandmother, mother, and I putter in the backyard garden, watering rose bushes and weeding cucumber and dill plants. There are red-brick houses on either side of my grandmother's house and another across the green chain-link fence. All of these square, neatly built brick homes have tidy rectangular gardens. My grandmother's garden is by far the most elaborate, the lawn bordered by purple pansies and wisteria that hangs from the side of the garage, profligate rose bushes and wide-leafed lilies, luxurious bursts of primroses and extravagant groupings of tropical birds of paradise that my grandmother has coaxed to full-bloom. The vegetable patch is there, of course, but tucked behind the garage, semi-obscured from the kitchen window.

My grandmother stands in the centre of the garden, surveying her small plantation, her face as close to contentment as I have seen since we arrived. Meanwhile, my mother and I sweat in the vegetable patch, pulling small prickly weeds from where they menace the white bulbs of the green onions.

Across the way, the neighbours sit at their picnic table, a rounded older couple in matching orange floral shirts. They wave enthusiastically at my grandmother and she raises her arm in greeting. "My daughter and granddaughter," she yells across the neighbours' impressive legion of tomato plants, "from British Columbia." My mother and I stand and wave and we all make happy noises. Then, greetings accomplished, my grandmother and her neighbours go back to politely ignoring each other. My mother and I kneel back down into the dirt.

"They've certainly gotten friendlier," I say in a low voice.

"What do you mean?" my mother asks, pushing her hair back under a yellow ball cap that belonged to my grandfather.

"Those were the neighbours that complained about me and Tara and Laura and Deidre swimming naked in the kiddie pool." Even as I say this, I realize the ridiculousness of this thirty-year grudge.

My mother shakes her head. "Different neighbours."

"What?"

"Different house. That was on McLeod Road, before Baba and Didi moved here in '87."

I look at the back at the house, the trim lawn, the white and red roses climbing the garage trellis. I had located this memory here, but my mother is right: the wading pool was in a similar but fundamentally different backyard. I shake my head, clearing it. Twice today I have been dislocated and I begin to feel an odd tilt to the progress of the afternoon.

"These neighbours nice," my grandmother says, overhearing us. She is wearing a white bonnet and gardening gloves, her full cul-de-sac regalia.

"They Italian," my grandmother continues. "From Sicily. Only grow tomatoes, that's all, all summer. Can them and make sauce from, eat all year long. Kids come for dinner every Sunday."

My grandmother gives us a dark look.

"Too bad you move so far," she says, turning her head to gaze at the tomato plants across the fence. "Maybe would be better, we Italian."

June 2011
Niagara Falls, Canada

AT BEDTIME, I SIT ON THE edge of the double mattress of one of the two guest bedrooms. Across the hall, I can hear my mother take on my grandfather's role, trying to buoy my grandmother out of the darkness that often consumes her before bed. "Good night, Irene. Good night, Irene, I'll see you in my dreams."

On the dresser across from me sits a hand-painted matryoshka doll. It is the same one my cousins and I played with as children, blithely scattering pieces under the couch and corners of the rec room. At some point, my grandmother collected the pieces and brought the doll up to this bedroom for safekeeping, screwing the pieces back together as tightly as she could. It is now almost impossible to open.

My mother opens my door for another chorus, clowning and off-key, blows me a kiss, then closes the door with a wink. She has one last exchange with my grandmother, the low, muffled tones of my grandmother's long day, the lighter, cajoling staccato of my mother's. There is a clink and then two light thuds as my mother closes first my grandmother's door, then her own. I hear my grandmother sigh, my mother climb into the single bed beside the wall, the snap of the reading light.

Everything that is young in me suddenly feels riled up, restless in the darkness and humid air of the June night. I feel an odd longing for Vancouver, its cool air and mindless youthfulness, the brightly lit amnesia of the coast. I forget my ambivalence, that odd lack of gravity on the high-rise lined streets of the West End, that sloping road down to English Bay where the glare off the sand blots out everything but the parade of pleasure seekers. I wish for the gauzy vagueness of sleep that I know will not come. Anything to avoid growing questions about events and people beyond this house.

These questions are a form of agitation. They are also a betrayal. I know my grandmother has worked hard at her stories. I know deeply, that her set versions are, above all else, acts of preservation — repetitions that allow her to contain her nightmares, carefully edited sequences that spare us and spare her having to tell us. In other years, these redacted versions have been enough. But this year the cracks in these tales have created a certainty there is more.

I glance toward the door, measuring the distance that separates us. I listen for something, some kind of sign, my grandmother rising from her bed, which would be deterrent enough. But everything is still, just the sound of a suburb at night, flat and close. I settle into the lace-edged pillows against the headboard, pull my laptop over the white coverlet, press the on button. I start with the camps.

The foreign labour camps were not the same as death camps. Those deported for labour, and only labour, were relatively fortunate, though malnutrition and poor conditions meant death was not uncommon. Not all of those deported for labour were consigned to camps. My grandmother has said the camp guards called the labourers "nyedlud," the Ukrainian word for not-human, which I assumed was a slur. I am startled to learn that along with those who were Jewish, Roma, Black, mixed race, homosexual, or physically or mentally disabled, Slavs were officially considered "subhuman" by the Reich. As such, the Eastern workers were more frequently sequestered in camps than other foreign workers, partly to allay Nazi fears of miscegenation.

The Reich's racial hierarchy also applied to food rations: French forced labourers received a higher calorie allowance than the Polish, the Polish far too little but more than those who came from further east. Scandinavian labourers, who were considered closest to the ideal, ate poorly — but twice as much as the lowest groups. Unlike other "subhuman" captives, European Jews in particular, the Reich did not mark the Eastern workers for wartime extermination, though a mixed use of ethnic cleansing, forced labour, and selective Germanization were all part of the Reich's "Master Plan for the East."

Seeking a visual anchor for all of this, I search for images of the Leica camp. The photographs I find of the barracks are all postwar: indistinct images of a low building, a wooden door.

As I search, I find sources that show how Leitz Werke was enmeshed in the larger labour patterns of wartime Germany. On the loss of his German workers to the war effort, Ernst Leitz II built the original barracks for what he hoped would be paid civilian labourers from Italy. These men never arrived, and Leitz was sent a group of French POW forced labourers, whose time at Leitz Werke was marked by rebellion and escape attempts. Throughout the war, French and Belgian forced labourers were a continuing presence, and by 1943 they had their own camp called Stadion. The Eastern forced workers, who became by far the larger group, were segregated in their own camp called Lahninsel. By early August of 1943, records show that there were 568 female and thirty-five male labourers at Lahninsel, mostly civilian deportees from the Ukraine. The labourers made Leicas but also the navigation gear for V-2 rockets. The camps were contested space, neither completely belonging to the Leitzes nor completely under the control of the Reich. This contest shaped the labourers' everyday lives.

As I continue searching, I come across forced labour testimonial projects and among these stories I find two accounts by female Ukrainian Leitz labourers. Both support my grandmother's memories of difficult conditions but also the food, clothes, and radios Elsie

Kühn-Leitz brought into the camp. Realizing I have only a dim sense of what she looked like, I enter "Elsie Kühn-Leitz" into an image search. I find a black-and-white photograph of an attractive woman in her mid-thirties, dark-blonde hair pulled back in a bun, wide-spaced eyes, intelligent and alert. There is a wry humour in these eyes. A serious woman, amused by the world but finding its management requires a certain sternness. In the University of California library system, I find a record of her 1936 doctoral dissertation on the inequities of the German marriage contract.

Elsie Kühn-Leitz
(SOURCE: ERNST LEITZ FOUNDATION)

Eventually, I find a detailed article about the Leica camp in an academic database. The article provides a summary of an essay that Elsie Kühn-Leitz wrote about her war years. This summary, reinforced by what I have read and what my grandmother has said, creates a trellis for reconstructing three days in September of 1943.

September 8, 1943
Wetzlar, Germany

AS ELSIE DRESSES, HER MIND IS full but, she is glad to realize, clear. She runs a brush through her hair and pulls it into a knot at the nape of her neck. Every day has become an exercise in austere self-presentation. It is practical to make one's way around the camp as neatly as possible. But it is also a type of litheness she equates with accomplishing each day's work as efficiently and discreetly as possible. Finished with the wooden hairpins, she carefully sorts through the items on her dressing table, making sure each object she pulled out in getting ready is returned to its drawer in the mahogany box, the hairpins with the hairpins, the earrings with the earrings.

As she sorts, she thinks of the children at breakfast, their chatter, their laughing, fluid motions as they ate their bread and jam, the happy ebb and flow of silly jokes and minor squabbles, Karin's face bright with the new day, Cornelia and Knut in their school uniforms, a universe so normal it carries with it an aura of unreality.

Elsie looks into the mirror, reassures herself that everything is in place. She smooths her brown linen suit, the one she bought the day she graduated from law school. Despite its good lines and fine material, it is hardly worn. She had had the suit made by the best tailor in Munich, with visions of her role as a prosecutor. This was before the violent jurisprudence of the Reich had made the practice of law impossible both by sidelining women and through the dark turn justice itself had taken. But today, she has decided to wear it.

Elsie leaves her suite and proceeds down the stairway, hearing the movements and clatter of the staff as the day's housework begins. Already there is new wax polish on the banister, a familiar scent that this morning triggers a vague, persistent nausea.

As Elsie reaches the first floor, she slows in front of her father's study. She can see him at his desk through the half-open door. Still handsome, still possessed of that quiet self-containment that made him a "captain of industry," a "man who knew his own mind," as people used to say. It had always been her father's motto to act, always to act, to strike decisively before the moment passed. And so in the lead up to Kristallnacht, he had sent away as many Jewish employees as could be accommodated on ships leaving for cities that housed Leica's foreign branches. To keep up overseas distribution, he explained to Nazi officials. To bolster our reputation abroad. And the Nazis, ever concerned with Germany's reputation for strength and innovation, always in need of foreign currency, had waved these employees through as they boarded steamships with their families and trunks, contact names in their address books, new model Leicas around their necks.

This was before the officials began using their own Leicas to photograph the sick and starving in the Warsaw ghetto, in conditions the Nazis themselves had created: see — these Jews are vermin — look at them in their depraved condition! Or Heinrich Hoffmann, Hitler's personal photographer, carefully using his Leica to craft the image of the Leader: photographs of Hitler accepting flowers from little blonde children, a model of paternal solicitude; or here, Hitler reclining on a pastoral hillside, his faithful Alsatian at his side, a man at home in nature.

Was it this perversion of everything her father had built that had led to his withdrawal from the details of their daily lives? Or was it the weight of knowing production was now determined according to Nazi will, bombsights and propaganda cameras all so essential to Hitler's war? The deep, inescapable knowledge that slaves now made goods in their name, so lately produced by German workers with health benefits and paid holiday? Her father, Elsie knows, is a man of social objectives, a man who believed in contributing to the type of civilization one wished to live in. And where for Elsie the test of faith came from every foreign worker gaunt with malnutrition, every female foreign labourer brought to her office in the cold light of the morning, bloodied and vacant-eyed from a night of Gestapo sport, she knew for her father it was different. The Nazis had not just taken from him his ability to act, they had stolen his ideals, twisting the company into a producer of grief, making him a double agent against the foundational beliefs of his own soul. And it was that spiritual erosion, Elsie feared, as much as Nazi threats that her father might not survive. That her father had taken out party membership to camouflage his actions, he said, to maintain some control over the factory, was something Elsie still, now, could barely admit to herself.

Her father, she realizes, has seen her, and has read the thoughts written on her face. Elsie had always known she was her father's joy, the one with the ability to delight and amuse him, eclipsing the sober reliability of her brothers. She had been the female presence in the house after the death of her own mother when she was six, and now again after her father's second wife, Hedwig, had died the year Cornelia was born, both women concert pianists, both women younger than her father by several years. When Elsie was a child, a contented look would come over her father's face when she was there, practising a piano overture her mother used to play or reciting a prayer in church. And the days they had spent together had led to an uncanny oneness of mind, an ability to receive thoughts one from the other without speaking. Lately, though, he had become remote from her, and the openness in his face now, in the clear, unadulterated fullness of seeing her as he used to, causes her to step forward into the office, the argument of the night before almost forgotten.

"Elsie-Lein," he says, with effort. "What are you doing in the shadows?"

It is an old line between them, from when Elsie was a small girl and would wake up to watch the dawn spread its pink glow across the grounds from the dining room window. When her father came down in his suit, surprised to find his small daughter in her nightgown, her fingers pressed against the glass, he asked what she was doing.

"Waiting for the light to dance!" she answered.

That summer they spent many mornings waiting together, for the wild spark of light that would animate the dew on the grass and turn the garden into a shimmering, fiery fairyland.

Sensing the rare opportunity to have a buoyant, inconsequential exchange, Elsie opens her mouth to make her standard childhood reply, but stops when she realizes how ridiculous it would sound now, and anyway her father has already turned his head. She stands in the doorway for a moment, then turns to go.

"Don't forget," her father says.

Elsie gives a half nod, aware of the tension in her neck. She pauses a moment, but with no ready reply continues down the hall. In the dining room, a flash of red material like a cocktail dress makes her think of days the room was filled with food and music, dazzling debate and discussion, the young artists intent on making photography the next major art form. But it is only a dusting cloth laid across a chair by one of the servants.

From the still, watchful expression on Friedrich's face as he opens the car door for her, Elsie can tell that her father has already spoken with him and drawn him into the task of looking out for her. Since her mother's death, this is how her father had filled the gap: he had put himself at the centre of her universe and created a constellation of support from the household staff, Friedrich and Frau Vogel, and later, when she was a teenager, Frau Lichen. Friedrich, who had been with her father longest due to a heart condition that had kept him out

Elsie and Ernst Leitz II

(SOURCE: ERNST LEITZ FOUNDATION)

of both wars, had carried Elsie on his shoulders when she was a child, giving her that stratospheric lift that allowed her to pick the reddest and shiniest apple off the tree, the September sunlight flooding her eyes as she reached greedily through the leaves. Still now he is half-uncle, half-employee, his wry knowledge of her childhood exploits, his gruff affection and concern, always just beneath the surface of a polished, laconic professionalism.

Friedrich keeps his eyes on the road as they travel down the hill and Elsie is grateful. She cannot be watched right now. If only Hof had not come to the house. In the backseat of the car, Elsie finds herself once again in the confines of her father's study, called in after Hof's departure.

"You know Hof is — connected," her father says, his voice low and intent. "He is a man with friends. Against his natural inclination, I suspect, he made the trip from Frankfurt to tell me — to warn me, Elsie, that the Leadership is having new doubts about us. You know Hof is not an assertive man, but he demanded, pleaded with me, that you, in particular, remain above suspicion. That we adopt a period of careful quietness, as he called it."

The unfiltered fear in her father's eyes sends a jolt through Elsie, jumbling the parts of her mind she has attempted to keep separate, her father, the children, the camp workers, the appalling story of the Palm family: Frau Palm's threats of suicide in the face of the newly reintensified crackdown on mixed marriages, a friend, Frau Gerke, willing to travel with her in an escape over the Swiss border; Elsie's own involvement and hurried planning: the Swiss francs, the map, Frau Palm and Frau Gerke's stay with Elsie's aunt in Munich, the women's July trek through the mountains, the silence since which Elsie could only hope meant successful escape.

Her father clears his throat. "Elsie, we always knew this moment would come. And now we have reached this — inevitability."

For her father's sake, Elsie tries to see, but when she looks at the situation without their resistance, all she sees is a family that stood by, like so many others. When she looks at her father in this way, she sees the profiteering acquiescence that has dominated German industry since Hitler. And as she cannot look at her father this way, she looks at the floor.

"Elsie," he says. "Every name has its limits."

The words hit their mark. In all of her activities, Elsie has wagered on the prominence of their position, the importance of the factory. Before the war, these elements were crucial to the gravitational centre that had drawn artists and industrialists and politicians to the house, to the lively stream of food and conversation and ideas which, Elsie believed, were at the heart of human flourishing. And since the war, it was these same qualities, their name, that Elsie had counted on to create a barrier. At some level, she has always believed these protections would keep them safe, and this belief has been the cool, steady centre of her ability to act. Now she is less sure and the doubt itself is a terrible thing.

As the car reaches the camp, the stark sight of the barbed wire stretched tight across the fence posts forces Elsie to put these thoughts away. It is a reminder, to everyone, not just of human captivity but of the cost of human vulnerability, of the easy tear of human flesh. The Nazis are good at symbols. None of the subtlety of Goethe or Schiller or Mann. But it was the lack of complexity, their easy, brutal solutions that had appealed to a foundering nation. The clear repetition of simplistic messaging was keenly crafted to appeal to the basest impulses and, as Leica's marketing director had once commented in waspish admiration, a feat of advertising.

Friedrich guides the car through the gates and stops the vehicle in front of the factory offices. His face is expressionless as he opens the door, which Elsie recognizes as a skillful blind drawn over the substance of his thoughts. She gives him a small, pursed smile as she steps out, letting him know he is fooling no one, and his rueful nod in return tells her he is well aware but will worry about her anyway.

Elsie allows the guard to open the heavy main door and walks down the cold hallway to her office, a utilitarian room far from the comfortable office in the main building where she had once worked in the accounting department. This room is windowless and contains only two chairs, a desk and the filing cabinet. The filing cabinet contains lists and information, including copies of the files of the foreign labourers working in the camp. Elsie is employed by the Labour Front, formed by the Nazi Party to replace the trade unions, which has a brief to carry out a modified form of workplace oversight.

Elsie pulls out a stack of files, continuing her work from the day before in assessing workers' access to bathing facilities. It is a complaint that Elsie hears often through Maria, that the guards interfere with the women's access to showers. Elsie feeds a piece of paper into the typewriter and begins a report to the Labour Front. She adjusts the carriage and is about to start typing when there is a light knock at the open door. Elsie looks up to see Herr Barth, the camp's organizational director, standing awkwardly in the doorway.

"Frau Kühn-Leitz."

"Herr Barth," Elsie says, knowing he will not ask her anything until she makes some invitation, a habit left over from when the family had more to say about day-to-day conditions. Sighing inwardly, Elsie gestures to the uncomfortable metal chair in front of the desk. Herr Barth declines with a formal bow but steps into her office.

"We have had a request — that is to say, it has been decided that the very ill or female workers with child will be sent to the repatriation camp at Pfaffenwald. The determination is that the medical facilities are much better equipped to handle such situations."

"I see," Elsie says, more to give herself time than anything else. Surely Herr Barth must be aware, as she is, of the rumours surrounding these repatriation camps, the same kind of uneasy speculation that has begun to mount about Jewish camps, from which emaciated prisoners in striped uniforms are sometimes released to clear the rubble after bombings, one of the few times they are seen on the outside. Elsie chooses her words carefully. "Of course, in so far as those decisions affect women in the camp, they need to be approved by you as camp director and me as subleader."

"Ah yes — of course," Herr Barth says uneasily.

"How many would be affected?"

Herr Barth takes a moment to consult the file under his right arm.

"At the moment, well, right now at least, it would seem only — well, two. Two women with tuberculosis would, er, the officials say, receive better care in a more established facility."

Elsie cannot argue that the sick could use better treatment than their makeshift clinic provides. Braun is a reasonable man and a decent doctor, but the clinic is forever understaffed and undersupplied. But the unusual nature of official concern for the welfare of the foreign workers makes her hesitate.

"Well, then. A visit seems in order."

"A visit?"

"To see the medical facilities. At Pfaffenwald by Vogelsberg."

"Er —"

"Tomorrow? If you would come by the house at seven-thirty we could get an early start."

"Certainly," Herr Barth says, nodding. "Yes, by all means. I will arrange it."

Herr Barth wavers for a moment in the doorway before backing out of the office. Elsie is still staring at the empty doorway, trying to make sense of the policy change, when Maria, the women's liaison, appears. With her blonde ringlets, efficient cheerfulness, and excellent language skills, Elsie is often at pains to remember that Maria isn't German.

"Another day," Maria says lightly, walking into Elsie's office and standing casually in front of her desk. She looks down at the sheet of paper in Elsie's typewriter. "Is that the report on showers you are working on?"

"Yes — we'll see what good it will do."

"You might add it's not just access. The girls say there's often no soap when they do get there."

Elsie nods and makes a note.

"How are things in the kitchen?" Elsie asks.

"The calorie count has been increased with the potatoes you had added to the soup, though it stinks as much as ever." Maria shrugs then continues. "The radio you brought in is popular with the women in dormitory four."

"They are keeping it well hidden during the day?"

"Everyone knows it would be confiscated."

As Elsie nods, she notices the shirt Maria is wearing. As a liaison, Maria is allowed to wear civilian clothing, among other privileges. Maria laughs.

"Thank you for this. I love the colour."

"It looks wonderful on you," Elsie says. And it is true. Even in the dim office, Maria glows with vitality, her blue eyes and blonde hair set off by the shirt's vivid blue.

"Maria," Elsie says after a moment. "Have you heard anything about the repatriation camp at Pfaffenwald by Vogelsberg?"

Maria's ability to gather information from the workers and guards is one of the things that makes her invaluable. But this time, after a pause, Maria shakes her head. "What should I know?"

"Nothing particularly. Herr Barth and I are making the trip tomorrow."

Maria raises her eyebrows, indicating that it will be a long journey. Elsie swallows a smile. Maria turns toward the door, waves cheerfully as she turns into the hallway. After checking it is empty, she turns back one last time.

"Heil Hitler," she says wryly.

"Goodbye, Maria," Elsie says, shaking her head.

September 9, 1943
Pfaffenwald by Vogelsberg

ELSIE LOOKS OUT AT THE PASSING greenery while Herr Barth drives. Before the war, this area was known for its hills and meadows, a place you would go for a weekend with friends, those kind of laughing adventures marked by good meals and long walks in the country. Once, when they were still in their twenties, she and Kurt had come for a long weekend with another couple, friends from the university, and stayed at a little inn by the river. Each day they had gone hiking in the hills, Kurt leading the way, pushing them forward until they had collapsed on the hillside. Elsie had spread out a checked cloth and Berthe, Elsie's friend from a political science course, had removed the contents of the picnic basket packed by the dour wife of the innkeeper. Elsie remembered Kurt standing on the hillside, throwing stones toward the summit, looking tanned and strong. She remembered Berthe's exclamation of surprise when she discovered the sandwiches were made from the entrails of the roast chicken the innkeeper's wife had served for dinner the night before. Some people, Berthe said, had a way of making their resentment felt. At the time, warmed by the summer sun, they thought it was a joke.

Now Elsie wonders if these fields might have been the ones traversed by Frau Palm and Frau Gerke on their way to Switzerland. She remembers the fevered look of Frau Palm's heart-shaped face the night before the journey south, the urgent pulse in Frau Gerke's stout fingers as Elsie had pressed the francs into her hand.

Herr Barth nervously downshifts as they take the turnoff that leads to the repatriation camp. In the year since he took on his role at the camp, his moustache and fine reddish brown hair have thinned, showing patches of pale skin beneath. The drive to Pfaffenwald from Wetzlar had taken more than four hours, slowed by Nazi checkpoints and the inevitable folding and unfolding of papers, the shuffle and bark of soldiers, men inflated by their power yet still retaining old habits of deference in the way they handed back her documents, careful to keep their gloved hands well away from hers. Herr Barth saw each checkpoint as reason to turn back, glancing nervously between his passenger to the stop point ahead.

"Our business is legitimate, Herr Barth," Elsie reassures him, wishing she had asked Friedrich to drive.

As the car nears the camp, Herr Barth looks over at Elsie. "What do you think we'll find then?" he asks.

"I don't know, Herr Barth," Elsie says. And thinks: *That is why we are here.*

Herr Barth begins to sweat again as a guard approaches the car. Haltingly, Herr Barth explains their business and, after consulting with a superior, the soldier motions to them to park outside the gate. Before Elsie can open the door herself, a tall, beefy camp officer opens it for her.

"Welcome to Pfaffenwald, Frau Kühn-Leitz," he says, with civility. "My name is Weber, the camp leader here. I trust you will find the tour of our facility informative." Weber is a type Elsie is familiar with, a Nazi yes-man, the kind who will expound on the values of common decency while taking secret satisfaction in the brutality of the Reich. These men give themselves away in their pseudo-military bearing, the closely cropped hair and snake-smooth skin, the look of never having missed a night's sleep.

"I understand," Weber continues, "that some of the Leitz Werke foreign workers, those unfortunately too ill to perform their duties, will be transferred here shortly?"

"That is a possibility," Elsie says.

"Yes, but then again, these things aren't always up to us?" Weber asks. When Elsie looks at him sharply, he adds smoothly, "Of course, I am only a camp employee, and make no pretense of being able to control more than my own small domain. And even then . . ." Weber lets the sentence trail off as he nods at a camp guard to open the door of the nearest barrack.

Sensing a signal passing between Weber and the guard, Elsie gestures to the adjacent barrack. "I think, if you don't mind, Herr Weber, Herr Barth and I would like to see that building there, please."

They wait for a suspended moment. And then an odd smirk crosses Weber's face as he pivots to the left.

"Certainly, Frau Kühn-Leitz," he says. "As you wish, of course."

Elsie senses the question mark in the guard's demeanour. Herr Barth clears his throat.

"Hein," Weber says to the guard. "Take Frau Kühn-Leitz where she wishes to go." Then, with a slight, ironic bow, "You will excuse me from accompanying you further, Frau Elsie. Herr Barth?"

Elsie recognizes, as she knows Weber intended, the familiar name she permits with staff and the women in the camp. It is clear that Weber had received a thorough briefing before their visit. Elsie nods at the guard, who leads them to the barrack Elsie had pointed out. He removes a set of keys from his belt. *They are locked in,* Elsie has time to think, before the door swings open.

The scene before them is so very like Brueghel's portrait of hell. The inside of the barrack is one large room, and it is the fetid odour of unwashed and frightened humanity that first overcomes her, the smell of something dirty, sweet, and festering. Living skeletons, men and women alike, languish on bare, stained mattresses that litter the floor. The flies are everywhere, landing on the mouths and eyes of unseeing bodies too weak to swat them away. The faces that are able to look up at Elsie are crazed. Ravaged bodies clothed in rags reveal emaciated femurs and ribs showing through translucent skin that seems barely able to contain them. The guard steps back, a hand covering his nose and mouth, and Elsie's first reaction is to follow, but she makes herself step inside and, with gratitude, realizes Herr Barth has done the same. Inside, the smells of filth and urine and decay become more distinct. Elsie counts at least three dozen bodies crammed into the room. An old woman lies on the mattress closest to the door, though as Elsie stares at her she realizes she isn't old, perhaps only in her late twenties, but emaciated with hair turned to white straw. The woman manages to grab hold of Herr Barth's brown sock. To his credit, Herr Barth does not pull back but rather crouches down to catch the woman's low and insistent words. Elsie scans the sunken faces and brittle bones of the people lying in such a desperate state. Acutely aware of her own helplessness, Elsie backs out the door, Herr Barth following behind her.

The guard stands outside. Elsie has an urge to smack the smooth blankness of his face, but instead clenches her arms against her sides.

"I want to see the kitchen," she says abruptly. The guard, retaining his show of impassivity, sets out for the camp's northeastern corner.

Elsie puts her arm on Herr Barth's to hold him back a little and feels a tremor beneath his suit jacket. Mindful that everything the guard hears will be reported back to Weber in ways that might have consequences for the workers, Elsie keeps her voice low.

"What did that woman say to you?"

Herr Barth pulls at his moustache for a moment and then says in a barely audible voice, "Her German was quite broken but she said — she said not to believe a word Weber says. She says five or six die every day — the guards bury them in the woods."

Elsie feels the last thread of doubt tear inside her. She knows, with sudden sureness, that the rumours must be true, that the worst is true, not just here but throughout the Reich.

As the guard leads them into the kitchen, a dirty shack at the far end of the camp, Elsie is overwhelmed by the rank smell of rotting vegetables. The guard leads them to a large, soft-looking man in a grimy apron, who is smoking in a corner otherwise filled with withered potatoes heaped on the ground. A metal pot of broth steams on a makeshift stove. The cook looks at the visitors through narrowed eyes, stirring the pot with a large spoon now and again, the cigarette ash falling into the pot's murky contents.

"What do these people eat each day?" Elsie asks him.

The cook flicks his eyes over to the guard, who gives a half-shrug. "Half a litre of soup at lunch and dinner, a bit of bread if we have it."

"How many in the camp?"

"Four to five hundred. Depends."

"And what if someone requests more?"

"No business of mine. I make it, they trade among themselves. The Ivans don't have a lot of morals where bread is concerned."

Unable to think of anything else to say in the face of such blatant lack of interest, Elsie turns to the guard.

"Where are the medical facilities?"

The guard says nothing, clearly indicating that there are none. Elsie sighs. "Show us the rest then."

In each quarter, it is more of the same — filthy latrines, bunkers filled with human despair. Where there is a German speaker, Elsie asks questions.

"Where will you go from here?" Elsie asks a man in his fifties who is leaning against a wall, his clothes reduced to a sagging uniform and one shoe.

"I don't worry too much, Madam," the man says gravely. "The authorities will send us home eventually."

In his resignation, Elsie recognizes an extreme version of the strange faith she often witnessed among the Leitz foreign workers, that need to believe that careful, steady endurance will outlast whatever dreadful circumstances. Their current incarceration is just one more version of something they have seen before, survived before, if only they put one foot in front of the other every day and wait until the sum of those days leads to some change. To complain, to protest, is not only dangerous, but a waste of valuable energy that might be conservéd to survive.

When the tour ends and the guard leads them back to the gate, Weber is nowhere to be seen. Another guard, perhaps seventeen and awkward in his uniform, opens the gate. Elsie and Herr Barth silently step outside the camp into the lush world beyond, the obscene, fresh green of the forest. Unable to stand, Elsie sits on a fallen log, considering the profane natural beauty that houses such utter human baseness. For a long while, she stares blindly into the woods. Finally, she looks over at Herr Barth, standing with the look of a baffled schoolboy, staring up into the grey sky.

Grimly, silently agreeing that there is nothing else to do, they climb into the car, which Herr Barth reverses with surprising force, then pulls around in a wide U-turn. As Elsie looks back at the camp, she sees Weber standing behind the crossbars of the gate, arms across his chest, watching them depart. At the sight of him, her numbness transforms into a cold, rigid loathing. She begins to trace every detail, every violation she will include in her report to the Labour Front.

September 10, 1943
Wetzlar, Germany

AT 6:30 A.M., ELSIE WAKES TO Heidi's hesitant hand on her shoulder. At first Elsie is annoyed. It is early; she does not want to wake the children; Heidi always did have a taste for the dramatic. Her mind is still full of her report on the repatriation camp, now sitting on the corner of her desk. She was up late committing the details of what she had seen to paper, fuelled by the intensity of her desire to send the report out today, no later than this afternoon. She feels grainy and indistinct in the face of the early morning intrusion.

As she focuses in on Heidi's pale, frightened face, however, Elsie sits up.

"There is a guard from the camp, Frau Elsie," Heidi says. "Downstairs. I told him it was too early, but he insists."

"Yes, coming," Elsie says, motioning Heidi out of the room. She dresses quickly, uncertain what the guard's visit could mean. She walks quietly past the children's rooms, smoothing the lines in her skirt as she descends the staircase.

The guard is standing in the entry hall, uneasy under the high ceilings and elaborate wood panelling. Elsie recognizes him as one of the gate guards of the Leitz camp, the one who often seems to be somewhere else, pale and dark, quite unlike the others.

"Yes, what is it?"

"It is Maria Holliwata," the guard says. "She is dying."

Having delivered his message, the quiet guard leaves. Elsie gathers her purse, coat, and gloves and is relieved when she finds Friedrich already in the garage. As they drive down the hill, the sun is rising over the town, lighting the spires of the cathedral. As they drive, Elsie is inundated by a series of images: Maria sitting laughingly in her office; the afternoons walking together as they made the rounds of the camp; the hours after work, when Maria would share the camp gossip, her skillful mimicry of various officials adding a spark to days that were often grey and indistinguishable. Elsie can think of no disease that would fell a woman in good health so quickly. She turns cold as she considers the possibility of cholera, said to be travelling west with the Eastern workers. But she puts that thought aside, unwilling to consider what this would mean for the crowded camp and for Wetzlar.

At the camp, Elsie directs Friedrich to the far end of the barracks, the ones near the field. Already the labourers are at the factory and the grounds are quiet. When Elsie enters the dormitory, she sees Herr Barth at the end of the hall, standing with a guard outside Maria's room. Even from a distance, Herr Barth looks crumpled. He issues some instructions to the guard, who nods and walks away as Elsie approaches. The room had been specifically assigned to Maria and, unusually, contains only one bed. There is a metal cabinet and a makeshift line from which Maria hung her clothes. Elsie recognizes many pieces from her own closet, the blue blouse among them. The bed is empty, stripped of its sheet and regulation grey wool blanket.

Elsie stops, taking in the empty scene.

"Yes," Herr Barth says, reading the question in her face. "She died not more than twenty minutes ago."

"She was ill?"

Herr Barth exhales deeply. "Very suddenly." And then, in a low voice: "The circumstances are unclear. She was fine yesterday and made her evening rounds as usual. She took ill early this morning and managed to call out to one of the women in the next room, who went to fetch Dr. Braun at the clinic. But Braun was detained by business outside the camp this morning, and by the time he arrived, it was already too late." Herr Barth takes a step closer until his mouth is very near Elsie's ear. "Among her belongings we found an official pass. For travel to Frankfurt. Without restrictions."

These final words are like an electric shock. Labourers, even those with elevated status and responsibility like Maria, are only allowed restricted movement, rarely outside of the vicinity of the camp, and only at certain times. Only a Gestapo informant would have something as valuable as an unrestricted travel pass. Elsie looks into Herr Barth's eyes and sees that he has reached the same conclusion. Elsie casts her mind back. Had she said anything compromising? Maria had exerted tremendous appeal, but no, she was quite certain, she had revealed nothing worth reporting to the Gestapo. Had she? But of course Maria had known about all the extras Elsie had delivered to the camp, not just food but also clothes. And the radios.

"I will make the funeral arrangements," Elsie says. "The best thing will be to proceed as normally as possible."

Herr Barth nods, turning in the direction of his office. Halfway back to the car, Elsie is intercepted by Inspector Mauer, tall and distant in his Gestapo uniform.

"Frau Kühn-Leitz."

"Inspector Mauer."

"I understand there has been a death, one of the Eastern workers, a leader in the group."

"Yes. Maria Holliwata died this morning."

"We will require all of her belongings, particularly her diaries."

"I don't know that she kept a —"

"She did," Mauer says with finality. "It would have been advisable for you to listen, Frau Kühn-Leitz, when I told you to keep your distance."

Mauer nods and looks toward the station house. After a moment, he says: "We will require those diaries by 8 a.m., Frau Kühn-Leitz. My superiors will not tolerate delay. In any event, I have been told to inform you that you must report to Gestapo headquarters at two o'clock for an interview. The same messsage has been delivered to Herr Leitz."

Elsie looks at her watch, a slim gold timepiece. It is seven-fifteen. Mauer looks at her for a long moment. Elsie nods at him, then returns to the car where Friedrich is waiting. As she approaches, Friedrich moves to open the door, but Elsie stops him with a hand on his arm.

"Go to the office," she says quietly. "Find Herr Barth. Have him remove every reference to me from Maria Holliwata's diaries. I have an interview with the Gestapo this afternoon."

Friedrich assimilates the gravity of her request and nods.

Elsie looks toward town. "I am going into town to buy a shroud and then to the church to see Pastor Gregor. When you have finished, come and get me."

A good deal of the morning Elsie spends inside the church, speaking with the pastor. It is an urgent, strained discussion masked by the organist's relentless rehearsal of *Jesu Meine Freude*. Elsie tells the pastor everything he may need to know. The music moves through the air like smoke, drifting up into the white coffers of the cathedral ceiling.

At two o'clock, Elsie and Herr Leitz report to the old building on the edge of Wetzlar that has been transformed into Gestapo headquarters. Red banners hang from the windows to the ground on either side of the main doors. It is a dark building with a cold stone façade Elsie has loathed since she was a child. The banners with swastikas are no improvement. Inside the reception area, it is oppressive and smells of disinfectant. A young officer rises from his desk and points out a metal chair to Elsie. He leads Herr Leitz to an interview room at the back of the building.

Elsie waits for two hours that feel like the passage of the night. When her father emerges from the back of the building with a young officer, his face is bloodless. Elsie stands to go to him but the officer intervenes. "You are wanted next."

Elsie is ushered into the same room at the back of the building. Another metal chair sits across a table from two Gestapo officers. The pebbled silver buttons on the black uniforms in front of her are bright under the glare of the overhead bulb. The door closes behind her. *A room without escape*, Elsie thinks, then tries to quell this thought. She has prepared careful answers about her relationship with Maria. She will suggest the woman was unstable, delusional. It will be her word against that of a Slav, and she knows that the regime's own hierarchy will work in her favour. By five o'clock, this could all be over.

The officer across the table, the slightly older of the two, begins the interview. He has smooth hair and movements and at first there is something incongruously benign about him, like the dentist she saw as a child.

"I am Inspector Gabusch, Frau Kühn-Leitz," the officer says with politeness. "You will be so kind as to answer a few questions, to clear up the matter at hand."

He waits for her to respond, and Elsie does, though her face and lips feel swollen.

"Yes, of course."

"You are Elsie Kühn-Leitz."

"Yes."

"Your father is Ernst Leitz, Jr."

"Yes."

"Your husband is Kurt Kühn."

"Yes."

"An officer in the Wehrmacht."

"Yes."

"You yourself are a subleader in the Leitz Werke camp."

"Yes."

"It is a position you sought out yourself."

"Yes."

"You were acquainted with Maria Holliwata."

"Yes — she worked under my direction in the Eastern workers' camp."

Each question is timed, a ruler hitting the table. *It is a rhythm*, Elsie thinks. *I am being lulled by rhythm.*

"And how is it that you know Frau Palm?"

The rhythm falters.

"Come now, Frau Kühn-Leitz. You remember Frau Palm, the Jewess you assisted in an escape over the border and her companion, Frau Gerke. They were caught at the border in July and have been in the Gestapo prison in Frankfurt. Frau Gerke denounced you last week. She accuses you and your father of pressuring her into the escape. She says that you forced her complicity — that it was you who arranged every detail."

Elsie lurches from the certainty this is about Maria into a new realm of fear. The professional aura has faded from the inspector's demeanour, revealing something much harder. Still, he retains a patient tone.

"One of the dangers of involving yourself with subhumans and their abettors, Frau Kühn-Leitz, is that they have neither intelligence nor loyalty. They are worse than animals. The two women got lost, stupid creatures, and hailed a passing milk truck — was it a milk truck?"

The other officer consults a thin folder. "Yes — a milk truck."

"Hailed a milk truck — to ask for *directions*. As a good citizen of the Reich, the driver reported them at the earliest opportunity. They were arrested shortly after. Frau Palm, we hear, is in poor condition, having decided to maintain her silence. But Frau Gerke has proved most pliant during interrogation."

His eyes still on Elsie, Gabusch removes a folded, multicoloured piece of paper from the file in his colleague's hands and brings it very close to Elsie.

"You recognize the map? Beautifully printed on expensive paper. From your father's collection, perhaps."

Elsie registers the dark-coloured mass on the familiar piece of paper in front of her as Lake Constance. More than five hundred kilometres long. Two hundred and fifty meters deep. She takes a breath.

"My father knows nothing about it. I take full responsibility."

"You do not deny these charges, then? You are accused of committing one of the greatest moral sins by supporting a Jewess, an archenemy of the Führer and the Third Reich. It is an action against the law."

"Against human law."

"You have broken — no, flouted the laws of the Fatherland. The ultimate law."

"God's law is the ultimate law, Inspector."

"You have abetted a subhuman in clear defiance of the Reich. And it is not the only time. We also have reports you have demonstrated excessive care for Bolshevik enemies in the Leitz Werke camp." *Maria. Maria at last.*

"All humans are equal under the law of God."

The inspector pauses, releasing air through his nose.

"Your position is unusual, Frau Kühn-Leitz. The Leadership would rather not see your family involved, out of respect for your father. However, these crimes cannot be overlooked."

Elsie closes her eyes and the interrogation room recedes. She tries to find something within herself to keep from screaming. It is Bach that comes to her, Bach against the rounded heights of the cathedral ceiling.

"I must inform you that you are no longer a free person. You will be transported immediately to the Gestapo prison in Frankfurt."

Elsie feels a flash of heat and bottomlessness. The dampness of the building seems to break through her pores.

"I need to see my family."

"You are too used to exceptions, Frau Kühn-Leitz," the younger officer says sharply. His anger is real and under much less control than the other officer.

"To say goodbye . . . please."

At this point Gabusch interrupts.

"Never mind, Inspector. Twenty minutes will make no difference to the guards in Frankfurt."

Aldefeldsche Haus, the Gestapo building in Wetzlar during WW II, photographed by Adolf Lux in 1935

(SOURCE: ARCHIVE RALF SCHNITZLER, COURTESY OF THE ERNST LEITZ FOUNDATION)

June 2011
Niagara Falls, Canada

WHEN I LOOK UP AT THE CLOCK, it is well past midnight. The air coming through the window has cooled and the house is quiet. Still lost in Elsie's story, I get up for a glass of water. The kitchen and hall lights have been left on, allowing me to see that my grandmother has turned the lock and deadbolt on the back door and fastened the chain.

I fill a glass from the pitcher and walk around the corner into the living room to find my grandmother sitting in the dark, watching a gameshow on mute. Her face is drawn and her cheekbones are high and prominent in the television's bluish light, her hair and ears hooded by a floral silk scarf, tied at the back. I am not surprised she is awake — we are all terrible sleepers, my grandmother most of all — but I am surprised I did not hear her get up and am anxious not to startle her.

"Baba?" I ask gently.

She looks over. From the remoteness of her expression, I can see she has not been watching the show at all. There is an inwardness that suggests she has been observing an entirely different scene, something far away and deeply private.

For a moment, I regret disturbing her and am struck by how small she looks, this elderly woman in her terrycloth robe, dwarfed by a stage set of thick beige curtains that cover the picture windows from end to end. But then something settles in the air between us, and I sit on the La-Z-Boy.

"You awake, Sasha?"

"Yes, you too."

"Yes," she sighs. "Nighttime always hard. So long the night."

She flicks the remote in her lap and the television screen goes dark. We are now lit obliquely by the kitchen light behind us. Somehow the dimness makes it easier.

"Baba, the Gestapo. They took Frau Elsie?"

My grandmother looks over at me, but not with any kind of surprise. There is weariness in her eyes and bitterness around her mouth, but no surprise.

"Yes. Was bad time. Very bad time in Germany."

"They came to the house?"

She nods, then stops, and a stillness comes over her body. She sits like that for a long time.

"Yes," she says at last. "One day they come."

September 10, 1943
Wetzlar, Germany

IN THE MORNING, WHEN IRINA LEAVES for the market, everything is normal. The children play outside with Heidi, enjoying the last of the warm autumn days. Herr Leitz sits in a wooden lawn chair with his newspaper, flipping through the pages. Frau Elsie and Friedrich are already at the camp. Frau Vogel reviews the foods in storage with Frau Lichen. Irina leaves them all behind when she rides her bicycle down the hill, the air full of the scent of sunshine on the grass and the last of the wild blackberries.

When Irina returns up the hill, the basket heavy with groceries, the first thing she notices is the quiet. The children and Herr Leitz are no longer outside. Friedrich has not returned from the camp to tend to the garden. As Irina rounds the side of the house to the kitchen door, she hears someone crying. Through the window she sees Heidi at the table, her face white against the background of green cabinets. Behind her, Frau Lichen is blank-faced, half a carrot in front of her, the knife cast to the side. Irina leans her bicycle against the door and hurries into the kitchen.

Heidi looks up. Against the whiteness, her face is stained with red patches.

"Frau Elsie and Herr Leitz are being interviewed."

There is no need to ask by whom. It is the sound of those boots on the driveway that Irina waits for, that she thinks she hears in the night when it is only raccoons or a deer. A pain begins to throb at the base of her neck. Frau Elsie has been taken for helping her, Irina thinks, and those like her in the camps. From the closed look that comes into Heidi's face, Irina knows she is thinking the same thing.

"We still don't know what all this is about," Frau Vogel says, aiming for calm. "It could be routine."

"They are Leitzes," Frau Lichen adds.

Irina drifts through the house. She feels frozen and disconnected from the rest of the staff who bundle together in corners of the house, from the bewildered children who react with uncertainty to the stilted quiet in the household and their mother's absence. At four o'clock, Irina takes a tray of cakes and cookies up to the children's room. Even without knowing what is happening, the children absorb the tension in the house and squabble over their games.

The children are in the bath when a car finally pulls up in the drive. Irina looks out the window and sees Frau Elsie, strained but straight-backed, emerging from the back of a black Mercedes. Friedrich pulls up behind, steps out quickly, and opens the door for Herr Leitz. Two Gestapo officers follow Frau Elsie up the stone steps. Irina hears the door open and a cry, possibly Heidi, a more muted exclamation from Frau Vogel. After a moment there is the sound of footsteps on the stairs, a rustle outside the door and Frau Elsie appears in the children's playroom. The children, hurriedly dried by Ada, tumble out of the bathroom and run to her.

"Mother," Knut says with seven-year-old exasperation. "Where have you been?"

"In town, Knut." Elsie kneels so that she is eye level. "I must go away for two or three days. I've come to say goodbye to you, just for now." Cornelia is quiet but tightens her grasp on her mother's shoulder. Karin nestles in between her mother's arms.

"Don't worry, my darlings. Be good." Frau Elsie's tone is light but Irina can see her falter as she kisses the children on the head, burying her face into their damp hair before pulling herself out of their grasp to head swiftly for the door, where two Gestapo officers now stand in their long coats. Karin begins to wail and Cornelia holds her tightly. Knut stares at the men, wide-eyed and puzzled. Behind him, the lined-up dolls stare blankly into the space where his mother was.

As Frau Elsie passes Irina outside the playroom door, she looks her squarely in the eye. In their depths, Irina sees defiance but also fear. Frau Elsie hurries down the stairs, the Gestapo officers behind her. The voices of the guards on the floor below become louder, and Irina hears Frau Elsie say "unnecessary," and an explosion of protest from Herr Leitz, followed by a short, aggressive response. The front door closes sharply. An engine turns over and car doors slam. A vehicle drives away.

While Ada tends to the children, the rest of the staff gather in the kitchen. For a long time, no one speaks. Then Frau Vogel says, hostility flaring in her eyes, "They brought her back just so the children would have to see her taken from the house in custody."

"No —" Heidi cuts in. "It means something that they let her come home to say goodbye. They wouldn't do that unless they planned to keep her under special circumstances."

Friedrich puts water on the stove to boil. From the sharp, clamped nature of his movements, Irina can see his mood has shifted from shock to rage. He stares out the window, as though willing the Gestapo guards to come back so that he can confront them, defend Frau Elsie, everything he thinks he should have done. Frau Vogel turns her head, shifts out of her chair, and hurries out of the kitchen, the first time Irina has seen even the smallest of crack in her decorous, professional manner. Frau Lichen presses an embroidered handkerchief against her cheek. After a few minutes, Heidi, wan and listless, leaves the room.

Friedrich makes tea for Frau Lichen, Irina, and himself. The three of them sit in front of their cups at the kitchen table. None of them drinks, though Irina uses the cup to warm her hands. The silence is broken by Herr Leitz, who appears at the kitchen door.

"Friedrich, I need you to drive." His manner is pressed but controlled.

Friedrich rises immediately, ducks out the kitchen entrance toward the garage.

After a few more minutes, Frau Lichen also stands, wipes away a few more tears, pours her tea and Friedrich's in the sink, rinses the cups, and leaves.

Irina is left alone in the kitchen, staring into her tea. She thinks about a woman in her village who used to read tea leaves. The woman was always busy, the villagers coming and going from her house, bringing pots of honey and loaves of bread in exchange for a glimpse into the future. Sediment and small pieces of the tea leaves have settled at the bottom of the amber liquid. They look murky and lifeless. They tell Irina nothing.

June 2011
Niagara Falls, Canada

THE NEXT MORNING, I WALK INTO the kitchen to find the vareniki project already in progress. I have come in with the intention of asking more about Frau Elsie's arrest, but the determined way my grandmother is rolling out the dough tells me she has stowed this memory firmly away like the sweaters she boxes with mothballs under her bed in spring. The vareniki, these small dumplings known in Polish as perogies, are a major undertaking, which is why my grandmother has started early. By the time I walk in at quarter to eight, the dough has already been made and left to sit in the fridge for an hour. My mother sits across the table, drinking coffee, wrapped in one of my grandmother's floral robes.

As I say good morning and pour myself a cup of coffee, I wonder which version of the dough my grandmother has made. There is a basic recipe, titled "varenky dough," written out on yellow paper for my mother when she moved west. In this recipe, my grandmother lists the ingredients in English but the instructions slip into Ukrainian. There is also a second version mostly written in my fourteen-year-old hand when I began to take an interest in transcribing as my grandmother cooked. This version is titled "vareniki," which appears to be written in an anglicized version of my grandmother's writing — though it could be mine. The rest of this recipe is in my writing, though my mother has made insertions at the bottom of the first page. Both sour cream and mayonnaise are among the ingredients, additions entirely absent in the first version. Other ingredients in this version include "2 cup warm milk," which is probably what my grandmother said, though there may be other places where I mistranscribed or misunderstood. It has crossed my mind to write a version C, a third and definitive edition, though I know these other recipes will always linger beneath its surface.

Baba's kitchen:
Summer visit, 1995 — Sasha and Irina

My mother clears her throat.

"So, Mom. Your famous vareniki. Better close the curtains or all those church guys will come around to ask you out."

My grandmother is nonplussed and takes it out on the dough, which spreads smoothly under the extra pressure from the rolling pin.

"You think you funny, Lucy. But when Pop die, all old widow men come around house. I have to say, 'Go away. Why you coming here?' What they think? I want to look after them? After all those years looking after Pop in nursing home? Twice every day I go to nursing home, look after him after stroke, take him good food. And before that, ten years I look after Korbans in nursing home, first him, then her. They help us come here, they have no children, have to do. She not so bad, but Mr. Korban awful, throw bedpan at nurses and call them communists. Terrible disease, Altimers."

I remember the violent lines of Mr. Korban's thin, insistent face and wonder how much Alzheimer's had to do with it. During childhood visits to the Korbans' living room with its overwhelming scent of air freshener, Mr. Korban's caustic comments were directed variously at Mrs. Korban, the Russian presence in Ukraine, and the newspaper delivery kids who brought the *Niagara Falls Review* at their peril. But for all of Mr. Korban's bombast, it was Mrs. Korban who frightened me most. During these visits, she would sit silently, hands in her lap, with an unnerving blue-eyed stare into the middle distance or fixed on my own face, her complexion floury under her grey permed hair and with the distant aura of someone not quite connected to this world.

My grandmother swallows, then coats the rolling pin with a thin layer of flour.

"Pop think maybe nurses communists, too, when he very sick," she says. "That why he no eat their food, think maybe they try to poison him. But he never throw bedpan at no one. He just wait for me to come every day with his borscht and his sandwiches. He wait for me every day. I only one for him and he only one for me. So after funeral I say 'go away' to those men from church. Disgusting how they come round so soon, looking for wife."

The dough rolled out, my grandmother straightens and wipes the flour from her hands. She shuffles to the cupboard and pulls out three water glasses, passes one to me and one to my mother. We each take a side of the kitchen table and press our glasses into the dough, making round cutouts with the open end of the glasses. My grandmother takes two bowls of filling out of the fridge — jarred black cherries, drained of their liquid, and mashed potatoes mixed with melted cheddar and small squares of caramelized onion.

We each begin stuffing the dough, two or three cherries to one varenik, fold in half, seal with the thumb and index finger moistened with water from a small china bowl my grandmother has placed in the centre of the table. For the potato stuffing, two teaspoons of filling are placed in the centre of the circle of dough and sealed the same way. The completed dumplings, fat little half-moons, are placed on floured baking trays, one for the potato, one for the cherry.

My grandmother's hands move quickly, her body relaxed and devoted to the rhythm of folding. I keep my eyes on the scalloped edges of the varenik in front of me. Hands covered in flour, I sort through what I learned in the night and try to square it with what I already knew. I press two ends of the varenik together, scalloping the edges with my fingers as the cherry juice bleeds into the dough, giving it a pinkish tint.

"So you were already at the Leitz house when you met Didi in the camp?"

Loss comes into the room like a breeze, the sudden image of my grandfather young and muscled. It hits my grandmother first and then my mother, who looks younger and more vulnerable in its wake. For a moment I regret the question. There is a pause and clatter as my grandmother transfers a baking sheet from the table to the kitchen counter and replaces it with an empty tray.

"Okay," she says, nodding slightly. "Okay, Sasha." These words tell me two things: it is all right I have asked and yes, she will tell me. My grandmother picks up her glass. "Is right that Didi and I meet when I was at Leitz house. We meet in camp. Not so long after they take Frau Elsie."

October 1943
Wetzlar, Germany

WHEN HERR LEITZ HAS HIS STROKE, it is the culmination of weeks of
tension. One moment he is in his study, raking through a list of people
who might help, the next he is on the floor, the left side of his face
a death mask. When he returns to the house from the clinic, he has
recovered much of his physical and mental ability, but the shakiness
and depression tell Irina things are still very bad.

Irina begins to spend her days off at the camp. She has the special
pass that Frau Elsie gave her that allows her to come and go through
the gates. She visits with her former roommates, bringing food from the
house. Occasionally, she goes by the clinic to help the women she used
to work with. One day, in early October, a trainload of male prisoners
arrives and she is pressed into service.

"Doesn't anybody ever check the ratio?" Doctor Braun mutters
as he directs the clinic workers to soak gauze in cool water and apply
salve and bandages. Irina washes down the ugly red blotches, the
familiar acid burns caused by the disinfectant. The men sit in rows

on the beds, and Irina moves from one body to the next, washing, dressing, washing, dressing, arms, legs, torsos. Confronted with a particularly badly burned back, Irina begins rinsing the wound with water. The man shudders and turns his head.

"Who's going to kill me first, you or the Germans?" Chiselled in profile, the man speaks to Irina in Russian, which she understands from school.

Irina is about to say something curt when she sees the whiteness of his teeth and realizes he is joking through the pain. Irina is struck first by the smile and then the features around them, the fine jawline and nose, the laughing green eye.

"Hopefully you will live," she says, keeping her eyes down, wiping down the tanned skin, taut with muscle, the edges of the burn.

The man looks over his shoulder at her as though she has said something funny.

"I hope so, too," he says.

As quickly and gently as she can, Irina applies the salve. The man begins to hum, something old-fashioned in a minor key. Irina finishes and moves on to the next man. From behind her new patient, she looks back at the green-eyed man and sees him gingerly pulling on his shirt, joking with another of the men. As he turns to leave, he looks over at her and winks. Irina busies her hands with bandages.

At the house, Irina continues to do the marketing, grocery items which Frau Lichen transforms into meals the staff, Herr Leitz, and the children eat without pleasure or comment. Rations become more strictly controlled and there is less variety. Each day, Irina collects as many items as she can find from Frau Vogel's list. The handwriting, which used to be direct and authoritative, becomes more spindly. In the afternoons, Irina polishes the silver and dusts the house. She brings tea to Herr Leitz, who sits on the loggia, staring into the garden. Heidi moves back to her parents' house in Lahnau and comes to work only in the day. Irina cannot blame her. Perhaps she would do the same if she had somewhere to go.

One warm evening in the middle of the month, Irina, Leah, and Marina walk down the hill to the camp for a special concert that has been organized by the labourers. There is a breeze that smells like fallen leaves and root vegetables. Below them, Wetzlar is spread out like a children's drawing of an ideal town: fields, houses, church, river, a cow wandering in the meadow.

"Do you think she'll come back?" Marina asks. It is the question on everyone's mind, but the one no one dares ask inside the house.

"Frau Vogel says the Gestapo consider Frau Elsie a dangerous example," Leah says. "Why would they release her?"

Leah and Marina move on and gossip about the others in the house and their acquaintances in the camp. When they reach the guard station, the three women show their papers and are allowed through the gate. They make their way to the central assembly area, where the concert will take place and a crowd has already gathered. No one is older than thirty. Together, the workers make up an artificial country of young, usable bodies. Irina tries not to think about what will happen if the war goes on, if these strong bones become brittle and weak.

A man Irina does not know, tall and thin, all kneecaps, forehead and Adam's apple, steps on to a wooden stage that has been tacked together. He promises them a night of song and entertainment. He keeps his comments neutral. There are guards standing at the far end of the yard. Irina is acutely aware of them, sensing their presence like heat on her skin. Two brothers take the stage and sing Ukrainian folk songs. Gradually, as the performance goes on, she loses her awareness of the guards, particularly when a group of teenage girls perform a lullaby her mother used to sing. The night ends with a comedy act, two jugglers and a woman Irina recognizes from her dormitory, Olga, the one with the overbite and her dark hair always in braids. With comic flair, Olga repeatedly bumps into the jugglers, causing them to drop the shoes they have kept rotating through the air. There is laughter from the crowd, cheers, a few good-natured taunts. This night of relative freedom is a luxury. The crowd savours it like a feast.

At the end of the night, the man who opened the show thanks them for coming and asks them to go back to their dormitories. The fact that they were able to get through the evening without interruption from the guards bodes well for the possibility of another event like this, and the spectators are careful, moving back toward the barracks with practiced efficiency, the men to the east side of the camp, the women to the west, sometimes a couple walking up the middle of the yard together, lingering for a moment, before breaking off in opposite directions. Irina looks around for Leah and Marina. She scans the stage area where the entertainers are putting away their props and small pieces of equipment. While she is watching, a man approaches. Irina recognizes the eyes first, green and laughing, then the smile. Without other men around, he seems less certain, less inclined to tease.

Female Eastern Forced Labourers
in front of barrack, 1943
(SOURCE: HISTORICAL ARCHIVE, CITY OF WETZLAR)

"Hello. Do you remember me?"

"Yes," Irina says. "How is your back?"

"Better. I wanted to thank you for helping me."

"You're welcome."

There is a silence.

"Would you like to go for a walk with me sometime?"

Irina considers this for a moment, wonders if this will be all right with the Leitz household. But Heidi has a boyfriend and their days off are unmonitored, their own.

"Saturday is my day off," she says, finally.

"I finish work at the loading dock at four on Saturdays. I could meet you here after?"

Irina feels unmoored.

"My name is Sergei," the man says by way of parting.

"I'm Irina," she says, feeling foolish not to have introduced herself before.

"I know," Sergei says. "I asked at the clinic before I left."

He smiles again and moves back into the crowd. Irina looks around and sees Leah and Maria standing by one of the outbuildings. She walks over and joins them.

"Who was that?" Marina asks. Leah giggles.

"Someone from the clinic," Irina says.

"He's so gorgeous," Marina says. "Are you going to see him again?"

Irina shrugs and looks away. Marina and Leah laugh. Irina points them in the direction of the gate. It would be better for them to go through sooner than later. The guards who are off duty drink at night and Irina doesn't want to run into them. They all feel more comfortable when they are on the road to Haus Friedwart, though Irina knows they could still be harassed by any of the townspeople who felt inclined to stop them. When she worked in the factory, townspeople would line the streets to yell "swine," at the Eastern workers, sometimes spitting on them or pelting them with stones as they walked back to the barracks after shifts in the factory. Irina has no interest in discovering what these same people might do in the night. She is surprised and relieved when she sees Friedrich along the side of the road, standing by the car.

"Get in," he says. "I told Herr Leitz you were out at the concert tonight and he said I should come get you."

Irina climbs gratefully into the back beside Leah. Marina, the first to settle into her seat, tucks her dark hair behind her ears and chats to Friedrich about the concert, relating the details of each of the performances. Irina half-listens to Marina's animated account, but as the car moves up the hill toward Haus Friedwart she finds herself back at the concert, speaking with Sergei.

June 2011
Niagara Falls, Canada

THE VARENIKI STOWED IN THE FRIDGE, my mother, grandmother, and I go grocery shopping in my grandmother's immaculate 1988 grey Oldsmobile sedan. My grandmother's list is long, divided by store, and written in English with a strong Cyrillic cast. The coupons my grandmother cuts neatly from supermarket flyers are attached to the list with a small paperclip.

We begin at Zehrs, where my grandmother picks through the bing cherries with practised hands. Her first job in Canada, the one Mr. Korban secured for her and for my grandfather when they first arrived in Niagara Falls, was picking fruit in Niagara on the Lake for ten cents an hour. The ability to sort the sweetest of the fruit has remained in her fingers, evident in the way she sorts with her thumb and forefinger, pulling only the roundest and firmest from the pile to add to her plastic bag. The cherries are also sold in green cardboard quarts, but these my grandmother dismisses.

"They make those for Angliski lyudi," she says. "English people always in a rush. Take packages the supermarket make, with sour cherry on the bottom. And then poof — they get them home and what they have? Sour cherry, mushy ones. Sometimes hard to understand what English people are thinking about. Always rushing. Eating Lean Cuisine like they see on television. What they do with time they save? Watch more television and eat sour cherry. What kind life is that?"

Beside us, a young man in his mid-twenties, blonde hair, red muscle shirt, picks up one of the pre-packaged cherry quarts and pops it in his plastic shopping basket beside a stack of frozen pizzas. My grandmother observes him darkly for a moment, looks knowingly at me, and continues raking through the fruit. The young man looks right through my grandmother, and she is careful to return his disregard. She knots the thin plastic bag full of cherries and places it on the kiddie seat of the metal shopping cart.

"Nectarine on sale, Sasha. Always your favourite. Go fill bag."

My mother joins us in produce and nudges my grandmother's backside gently with her cart.

"Ah, Lucy!" my grandmother exclaims. "What's the matter for you?" Something of the old feistiness returns and she looks challengingly at my mother. "So good you were until you were eight year old, always helping me with the house. But then what happen? You wear black all the time, start smoking cigarette."

"When you were eight?" I ask.

"Sixteen," my grandmother says. "You think I don't know? You and your friends go so wild, share cigarette in your room, spray Lysol all over everything when I come home from work all day at restaurant."

"Wild," I say to my mother, who actually giggles as she picks up something from her cart.

"But look what I got you now," my mother says. My grandmother peers at the package, suspicious.

"What's that?"

My mother grins.

"Twinkies."

My grandmother scowls, full of the certain knowledge that Twinkies are the apogée of North American decadence, all of its sins wrapped up in faux sponge cake and corn syrup filling.

"Ah, Lucy," my grandmother says, pushing her cart toward the checkout. "You trying to kill me."

At the car, my mother and I load the bags into the trunk beside my grandmother's cane. We take our seats, my mother in the driver's seat, my grandmother beside her, me in the back.

"See," my grandmother says, studying the bill. "With coupon, we save six dollar, eighty-two cent. Canada Day week sale."

My mother pulls the Twinkie package out from where she had it tucked under her arm. My grandmother looks up from the bill.

"No, Lucy," my grandmother says.

My mother rips open the packaging, tosses a wrapped Twinkie to me in the back. I examine the cellophane, shrug, and open the package, careful not to touch the Twinkie with my unwashed hands. I take a bite and am struck by the strangely appealing combination of sponge cake, fake cream, and artificial vanilla.

"Take one," my mother says to my grandmother, waving the package in front of her. "It will give you energy."

"I don't want none, Lucy," my grandmother says, shaking her head. "Give to kids when they come Saturday."

"You'd better have one," my mother says to her with mock seriousness. "Otherwise they'll go to waste."

"Oh, come on," I say, my mouth full of crumbs and filling. "Twinkies will survive the atom bomb."

But the word "waste" is more than my grandmother can handle. She removes a Twinkie from the package, as careful as I was not to touch the cake with her fingers. She takes a bite, turning the taste over in her mouth. She chews for a moment, swallows, looks at the hood of the red Honda parked in front of us.

"Not bad," she says.

In the end, the Twinkies are the highlight of the afternoon. From Zehrs we drive to IGA, from IGA to Sobeys. In each strip mall parking lot, we pull my grandmother out of the Oldsmobile and into the heat which rises from the tarmac. My mother pops the trunk. I fetch the cane, and we shuffle through the glass doors to be swallowed by the air conditioning where we collect the flyer items, go through check out, and are regurgitated back into the heat. We shuffle back to the car, I take my grandmother's cane, place it in the trunk beside the shopping bags, climb back into the car, drive, start again.

Sensing the chafe of our impatience, my grandmother studies the bill after each store, using her reading glasses to see the small purple print. "See? With coupon we save eight dollar, seventeen cent. Always worth it to go to all stores, not just one."

By the time we reach our last stop, my grandmother is tired and the glacial pace has put my mother and me on edge. "Why don't you stay in the car with Sasha," my mother says, making it sound like a question as she grabs the list and coupons from where they sit on the console and jumps out of the car before my grandmother can protest.

My grandmother pulls some twenty-dollar bills out of her handbag and waves them at my mother but it is too late "Lucy! Luuuuuucy!"

My mother grabs a buggy from outside the store and guns it for the entrance, her blonde hair swinging behind her. My grandmother puts the money back in her purse with a sigh and we stare blankly, for a while, at the bright yellow bricks of the No Frills store. Their slogan is painted in black block letters: "Take the frill out of your bill." The air conditioning in the car begins to wear off and the grey interior fills with humid air and the smell of newly laid asphalt.

"Good price, No Frills," my grandmother says.

"Yes," I say.

"Didi always like rye bread from No Frills. Good German rye. Roggenbrot. That German word for rye bread."

"Mmmmm."

"Today Saturday, Sasha?"

"No, Baba. It's Thursday. The lunch is Saturday."

"When we in Germany, Saturday was day I see your grandfather. Always Saturday."

October 1943
Wetzlar, Germany

SATURDAYS IRINA WALKS WITH SERGEI IN the fenced fields adjacent to the camp. Irina is surprised that they are allowed this freedom, but the guards are confident in their wire and their dogs. Irina is not sure how the first Saturday turns into a weekly event, but she is glad. She and Sergei walk through yellowing fields of grass, mostly along the river, the reflected lines of barbed wire wavering on the water. Irina packs picnics in the kitchen at Haus Friedwart, and they sit in the field and eat the good chicken that Frau Lichen has prepared, pressed onto slices of rye bread. Sergei eats with concentration, rolling a piece of chicken between his fingers before popping it in his mouth.

As they walk, they tell the stories of their lives and where they came from, she in Ukrainian, he in Russian, occasionally grasping for a different word when the other looks puzzled. Through the telling, Irina feels her limbs begin to warm, a melting of the frozen block in her chest. Her tongue feels as though it is recovering from frostbite, and she flexes it into the stories with a stiffness that gives way to

Leitz factory with labour barracks, Wetzlar, 1943

(SOURCE: HISTORICAL ARCHIVE, CITY OF WETZLAR)

gradual ease. She tells Sergei about Stanytsia and her family, about the time she and her cousin walked twenty kilometres with sixteen-pound bags of beet sugar on their shoulders to trade for salt, how they got lost on the way home in the dark, how frightened they were, how the bags left bruises the size of bricks on their shoulders. She tells him about the time she was ten and tried to get water from the well and fell in, saved by a passing neighbour. After several walks, she tells him about the day the Germans came, when they first surrounded the village, the tips of their guns visible over the top of the kalyna bushes.

When the soldiers entered the village, it was in a swarm. Their appetites were endless, for food, for violence, for women. As it became clear what was happening, many of the young women ran home and dressed in their mothers' clothes, hobbling around as if on ancient and aching bones. Sometimes the disguise worked and they were left alone. Sometimes it did not. Some hint of youthfulness, a vigorous stride, a smooth cheek, would betray these women and the German soldiers would strip them in the centre of the village.

"They had lists that the Collective gave them," Irina says. "They were very complete. Very official. The names, ages, and addresses of everyone aged fourteen to twenty-one. All neatly typed and handed over to the Nazis."

Through all of this Sergei listens, absorbing what she has to say as though he has an endless capacity to take it in. When he speaks, he tells her he was orphaned, his father dead when he was nine months old, his mother wasted by typhus, dying when he was three. He remembers clinging to his aunt's leg in the hospital when his mother was ill, too afraid to go to her before she died. That aunt took him in, but he was sent to another in Siberia when he drank a glass of milk the first aunt had expressed for her own baby. The second aunt kept him for a year but then, at age six, he was given to an orphanage and then a series of foster homes. He tells her about being fifteen and befriending a pair of pet mice. When the cat of the house ate the mice, he took his revenge by rubbing smelling salts under the cat's tail. It howled and jumped out the window, never to be seen again. He laughs until the tears run down his face when he tells this story. He laughs when he tells most of his stories. The only time he is grave is when he tells her about his mother.

"But how did you get here?" Irina asks.

"How did any of us get here?" Sergei waves his hand over the landscape. "By the will of the Deutschland gods."

He looks as though he might dodge her question, but something gives way. Irina knows how he feels. There is a relief in telling.

"First I joined the merchant marines," Sergei says, his hand skimming the top of the tall grass. "Sailing the Black Sea, Crimea, Volga. Then at eighteen, it was compulsory military service, and I became a lieutenant at the military college.

"I had my own unit, a small one, heavy artillery," Sergei continues. "I led a group to the front. We had nothing — holes in our boots, very little food. We tried to sing to keep up morale. You know 'Katyusha'?"

He sings a line and Irina nods. The melancholic melody is only distantly familiar, but she wants Sergei to keep talking.

"The German air force — first they would bomb us and then they would drop leaflets saying 'Russians, your air force is useless. Come over to the German side. We will give you food.'"

He gives a snort of disbelief. "Then they would shoot again. Sometimes the Wehrmacht made designs in the chests of the men, like artists, bullets around the heart. They were bored, I think, by how easy it was in the beginning."

Sergei picks up an unusual-looking stone on the path, weighs it in his hand, then begins rolling it over his fingertips.

"We were in a village near Kyiv when the Germans surrounded us. I found some civilian clothes on a laundry line and put them on, threw out the uniform but kept the gun. I was stumbling around, trying to keep low in the shooting when I found a trench. A woman yelled to me to get in and we hid there together. She was a nurse with another unit. Finally, when the shooting ended and the Germans took over, they shot the Russian soldiers they found, but they let the civilians go. They let me pass."

Sergei throws the stone into the woods, a tic troubling one of his eyes.

"The nurse asked me to walk her to her home about fifteen kilometres away, so I did. We kept being stopped by the Germans. At first, I hid my gun in a loaf of bread in her basket, but when they checked under the cloth once, I hid it in the back of my pants. We were stopped again and a German patted me down, but didn't find the gun. At another checkpoint, I accidentally looked a German soldier in the eye. He pointed to the body of a dead Russian beside him. 'You want to be like him?" he says to me.

"When the nurse and I reached her village, I hid with different families for a few months, working the fields. I just blended in there, until the Nazis came and swept up all the young people for labour. That's how I ended up here.'

He gives a little ta-da gesture, as though he has materialized through sleight of hand. He is clowning but for Irina it is like magic that he has appeared, that he remains. They walk for a while in silence, listening to the wind through the trees, the distant noise from the camp. Then Sergei takes Irina's hand and together they wade through the deep grass by the river.

June 2011
Niagara Falls, Canada

MY MOTHER EMERGES FROM THE GROCERY store with two bright yellow plastic shopping bags. Without breaking stride, she pops the trunk with the clicker, deposits the bags, and slides in the driver's side.

"Okay, Mom. We did it. But that's it, okay?"

"Maybe since we out, go to hardware store, get some —"

"No, Mom."

"Okay, then we just go by garden centre —"

"We're done, okay?"

This time it is my grandmother who concedes, though I can see her bite her lip and mark this concession on the running table in her mind. My mother starts the engine and pulls out of the parking lot into Lundy's Lane. It is nearing four o'clock and the road is busy. My mother adjusts her sunglasses, opens the sunroof, and looks sideways at my grandmother.

"You want to go for a ride, Mom?"

My grandmother stills for a moment then quickens. "Yes. Yes, I do."

"Ice cream?" It has been two hours since the Twinkies.

"Okay — but only if my treat."

We drive to a pick-up window further along Lundy's Lane and buy soft serve sundaes, butterscotch for my grandmother, chocolate for my mother, strawberry for me. My mother drives down toward the falls, past sparse clumps of tourists cooling themselves in the spray by the railings. "Used to be so busy this time year," my grandmother says, holding her cup of melting soft serve. "Where everybody go?"

We pass Harry Oake's mansion and the treacherous stretch of water where Bobby Leach launched himself over the falls in a barrel. In the distance, I can see the Rainbow Tower where Marilyn Monroe raced up the stairs in the fifties thriller *Niagara*. Beyond that, on Clifton Hill, sit the carnivalesque series of fast food joints and tourist shops and fun houses. I wonder if the little video-making place is still there, down a set of stairs from street level, lit in fluorescent pink lights, the studio where every year my mother, cousins, and I recorded terrible versions of songs by The Supremes, topping off the vocals with video-recorded air-band performances on drums, keyboard, and electric guitar, the irrefutable record of our collective lack of musical talent.

My mother turns right and down the giant hill to Dufferin Islands, and I can see her reliving it all: screaming her way down the hill on the handlebars of Alex's bicycle as a child, the teenage evenings cruising the strip, Saturday nights sneaking over the river to dance to the blues acts that would travel the circuit in Niagara Falls, New York. My grandmother rolls down the window to let the wind blow on her face.

We turn into rolling parkland and again into one of the parking stalls that face the water. Small manmade islands are connected by footbridges. Both the islands and the water are dwarfed by enormous swamp trees, willows with branches so long they sweep the surface of the placid water beneath. We sit in silence, revelling in the cool gloop of the melting sundaes. We are the only ones in the park other than an extended family who sit around a series of picnic tables farther along the grass. The mix of English and Punjabi floats along with the scent of samosas and chapati that fill large aluminum pans topping two of the picnic tables.

"Too polluted to swim now," my grandmother says. "You remember how busy used to be here in summer, Lucy. How much Pop like to swim after work at Norton Factory, shovelling coal on hot fire all day."

When I look up from the bottom of my sundae cup, my grandmother has fallen asleep, her head cradled between the grey seat-back and the half-opened window. My mother gently takes the plastic cup from her hand and gestures to me with her head. We step out of the Oldsmobile, lock the doors but leave the windows open, toss the sundae cups in a nearby trash barrel. It is pleasant and shady in the park, and together my mother and I wander over the wooden bridges between the small islands. The breeze off the Falls skims our skin, the willows, the surface of the water.

We pause at the apex of one of the bridges, watching the flow of the water beneath as I tell my mother about the story my grandmother recounted the night before. My mother already has many of these pieces. We compare, but still there is a feeling of incompleteness.

"What isn't she telling us?" I ask.

My mother's eyes are shaded by her sunglasses. But her upper body contracts in a quick, instinctive shrug.

"She was nineteen when she was captured by a gang of Nazi soldiers. There are things she's not going to talk about."

"I know," I say, weighing each word, trying to move carefully between my grandmother's privacy, my mother's protectiveness, and my own desire for something unnamed.

"I know," I say again, though I don't, not really. "It's just there's something very . . . contained about most of the stories she tells. And the emphasis is off. There's so much about food . . ."

My mother mulls this for a moment. When she turns to me, the sun falls directly on her face, and there is a tension between our habitual closeness and a rare, passing impatience with the way I am playing academic with stories so close to home.

"Well," she says, pushing back from the railing. "Maybe if you'd been hungry like that, your stories would be about food, too."

It is the sound of the Oldsmobile's engine turning over that wakes my grandmother, a red scarf lifted from a sari by a passing breeze that fixes her gaze when she opens her eyes. From her expression, it is clear my grandmother has stayed in a time when she and my grandfather were working, when their children were young. The Saturday night excitement has gone out of my mother's driving, but there is still a cool handling of the wheel suggestive of the easy ownership of the strip during her teenage years. I remember on a childhood visit we once rented yellow pedal boats to cruise along the river, but I see no sign of them now.

As we climb the hill and leave the tourist zone, the small houses on the way to my grandmother's neighbourhood are a blur of red brick houses, green lawns, and single-lane driveways. I lean my forehead against the cool glass of the backseat window, lulled by the steady count of houses, the distant smell of chlorine from one of the outdoor public swimming pools, the late-model Fords made at the nearby plant in Hamilton, many with rust spots from the road salt of snow-filled winters. I listen to the steady click of one of the Oldsmobile's tires. I think about what my grandmother told me the night before.

November 28, 1943
Wetzlar, Germany

THE FESTIVE SEASON APPROACHES, BUT THIS year no one washes and irons the Christmas tablecloths or pulls out the wide-ribboned bows for the staircase. Herr Leitz takes meals by himself, in his study, among a growing stack of books of Hoffmann photographs and Nazi propaganda flyers. On his desk sits the long list of the names of people who might be able to help Frau Elsie. Most of the names are scratched out. The staff eat semi-silent meals in the kitchen, a general grimness having settled over the house like grit. Irina watches Friedrich, Frau Vogel, and Frau Lichen out of the corner of her eye. *They have gotten older*, she thinks. Eventually, the lethargy becomes a kind of norm, and Irina becomes accustomed to going about the business of the day in a suppressed, underwater world.

One Sunday morning, Herr Leitz and Friedrich leave early for the Frankfurt jail. This is not unusual. Sometimes the Gestapo guards keep Herr Leitz waiting half the day before giving him some kind of update about Frau Elsie, and the anxiety of waiting pushes him to such nervous exhaustion that Frau Vogel often has Doctor Klein waiting on Herr Leitz's return. Today, however, the car returns early in the afternoon, and Irina wonders if the Gestapo have turned Herr Leitz away. From the window of the music room, Irina watches Friedrich move around the car with a stealth she hasn't seen in a long time. He opens the door, but it isn't Herr Leitz who emerges. It is a woman, thin and pale in a camel coat several sizes too large, her thin hair lank in the chill November air. Friedrich helps the woman from the car as though afraid she will break under his hand. The woman hardly seems to notice. She stares at the house as though doubting its existence. Herr Leitz emerges from the car and says something in the woman's ear.

All at once the quiet house is filled with motion, shouts from the staff and the sound of feet running down the stairs. Galvanized, Irina runs toward the front hall. The door is open, and Leah and Marina are hurrying onto the veranda. Irina, too, heads outside to find the rest of the staff already on the steps. The children hold on to Ada and stare with uncertain eyes at the thin, scruffy woman approaching the house.

At the bottom of the stairs, Frau Elsie slips from Herr Leitz's grasp and collapses. Raking the staircase with her fingernails, her eyes tracing the outline of each stone step, she begins to crawl. Overwhelmed, the staff, too, sink to their knees. Through their tears, they help Frau Elsie up the stairs, a hand here, pressure on her elbow there. Herr Leitz and Friedrich follow, a barrier to keep the crawling form from falling back. Knee after hand, Frau Elsie claws her way up the staircase. At the top, her body gives out, and she sinks into the stone, her cheek flat against the veranda, staring sideways at the house. It is Frau Vogel who helps Elsie to her knees and raises her up. For a moment there is no distance between the two women, just grey jersey against the folds of the camel coat. But then Friedrich and Herr Leitz press in behind, and the four figures disappear into the house.

June 2011
Niagara Falls, Canada

FRIDAY MORNING, TIME ACCELERATES, folds into itself like the linen napkins I smooth into quarters and place beside the good china plates on the dining room table. Beside me, my grandmother is quiet, running a yellow tea towel over the porcelain cups she uses for company. By the end of the morning, the table is set, and my grandmother wears a look of satisfaction.

"Better," she says, her mind already on the following day.

Winter 1943
Wetzlar, Germany

IRINA CLOSES THE DOOR TO FRAU Elsie's room and carries the tray down the stairs. In the kitchen, Frau Lichen examines the small bite marks in the half-eaten sandwich, the cold tea, the untouched biscuits.

"What does she do up there all day?" the older woman asks, shaking her head.

Irina does not know how to explain what she sees, the way Frau Elsie seems to have vacated the building of her own body, especially the days she is forced to return to Gestapo headquarters in Wetzlar for ongoing monitoring and interrogation.

"She listens," Irina says.

"What?"

"To her record," Irina adds. And this is true. When the children are at school, Frau Elsie spends much of the day listening to one movement on her phonograph. She listens and moves the needle back to listen again. It is from Tchaikovsky's *Swan Lake*, which Irina recognizes from her Russian culture course at the college in Kyiv. But even as Irina says this, she knows it is not quite right. It is true that Frau Elsie listens to the movement repeatedly, endlessly, even as Herr Leitz frets that the house is still being watched by the Gestapo, saying Frau Elsie should play Beethoven instead. But it is also clear that Frau Elsie is not really listening to the music but to something beyond it, a distant vanishing point well beyond what Irina can perceive.

It is two months before Frau Elsie ceases to play the record alone in her room. The version of herself she has performed for the children since her return becomes more natural and extends through more of the day. The hair that was shorn to rid her of prison lice begins to bloom around her face, thick dark-blonde tufts highlighted by grey. She returns to the lunch table, sitting quietly with Herr Leitz in the dining room. Dr. Klein's visits become less frequent. It is only then that Irina tells Frau Elsie about Sergei.

Frau Elsie arranges the wedding at city hall and is a witness at the ceremony along with Viktor, Sergei's quick, dark-haired friend with whom he makes deliveries for the camp officers. As part of the terms of her release, Frau Elsie is forbidden from entering the foreign labour camp. Nonetheless, she arranges for Irina and Sergei to have a room together in the camp, against the usual segregation protocol. When Sergei is away on overnight deliveries, Irina stays at Haus Friedwart.

On the evenings Sergei returns, they sleep pressed together on the single bed in their shared room. Burrowing into the leanness of Sergei's ribs, Irina listens to the camp noise or the drop of distant bombs. The vibrations travel through the darkness, move stealthily through the night. It makes it seem they are in motion, that the bed is a raft floating down a river.

June 2011
Niagara Falls, Canada

AFTER SETTING THE TABLE, my grandmother and I move on to cleaning the upstairs bathroom, sudsy water swishing along the edges of the tub as I rinse. At the sink, my grandmother rubs the already spotless mirror with Windex and paper towels. What I notice is how much time she takes, the purple veins on the back of her hand as it moves back and forth across the glass, the way she runs the paper towel through each groove of the water taps, then looks up again at the mirror.

Winter 1944
Wetzlar, Germany

IRINA SCRUBS THE STEEL CABINET, shakes out the grey blanket on the single bed, dusts the perfume bottle, the sharp edge of Sergei's razor. She cleans but really she waits, performing these chores to keep herself from thinking about waiting, without any certainty that she will be able to stop waiting, that what she is waiting for will finally happen. Waiting and cleaning have become a ritual.

One night much like this one, Sergei returns at two in the morning with eighteen bullet holes in the tail of his coat. He cocks his eyebrow at her, then sits on the little bed and laughs until she laughs too, her hand pressed against her mouth. Sergei laughs until the tears run down his face, then seeming to get ahold of himself, grasps her arm.

"You know Viktor and I were making deliveries to Braunfels."

Irina nods.

"We were carrying barrels of champagne for officers in the next camp. Of course the barrels look like gasoline containers, and the next thing we knew there were American planes overhead. I was riding in the back and saw them first, and I banged on the cab. Viktor pulled over into the bushes, and we jumped out of the truck into the woods. There were four planes. I saw them. There were bombs and bullets . . . the noise . . ."

The laughter seems to bubble up in him again but Sergei catches it in his throat, wipes his eyes. Irina holds his hand, anchoring him.

"The truck exploded into flames and there were streams of champagne shooting into the air, like a giant party."

Sergei swallows.

"I looked down at my hands in the dirt and see this."

He lifts his right arm from his thigh and shows Irina a bullet hole she had not noticed, one that has passed right through the wool of his coat. Only the light grey lining separates him from the bullet. Irina stands up and retrieves her sewing kit from the cabinet. With Sergei still in the coat, she tries to sew up the hole, but the material is shaking and she cannot seem to push the needle through the wool.

"Don't worry, Irina," Sergei says. "It was close, but I'm here."

It was close, but I'm here. Now Sergei is not close and he is not here and Irina is in their room waiting again. Three months ago he and Viktor were gathered up in a platoon of a thousand men to dig trenches against the advance of the Allies. They work under the supervision of guards who survey their progress with pistols and billy sticks. And so somewhere in the German countryside Sergei is lifting shovels of earth against the arrival of Americans. At least that is what he was doing. Since February there have been only rumours, fragments. An American air raid. A scattering of the work platoon. Missing.

Nightly she returns to their room to wait, to tidy what is already clean. When darkness sets in, she returns to Haus Friedwart, pushing her bicycle. There are no groceries in the basket. The bicycle should feel light but there is such heaviness Irina wonders if she will make it up the hill.

June 2011
Niagara Falls, Canada

SATURDAY MORNING, MY GRANDMOTHER DRESSES CAREFULLY in white slacks and a purple blouse with yellow flowers. She dabs on perfume, puts on her large gold Greek Orthodox cross and small pearl earrings. She counts the dishes in the basement fridge, meat on sticks, potato vareniki boiled and sautéed in butter and onion, cherry vareniki boiled and covered in melted butter and sugar. I notice another foil-covered pan on a lower rack above the watermelon.

"What's that?" I ask.

"Oh, just little bit cabbage roll I make this morning. Wake up early. Think maybe we don't have enough food for party."

My mother overhears from where she is ironing in the rec room.

"Mom, we don't need cabbage rolls. We have lasagna."

My grandmother pretends not to hear this and busies herself pulling out the spinach, onion, and potatoes to make mashed potatoes and cream-spinach in the upstairs kitchen.

"I make a cabbage roll casserole sometimes," I say gamely. "You just layer it up — cabbage, rice, tomato sauce. It's really quick when you don't roll each one."

A look of pain crosses my grandmother's face. She pauses, the vegetables in a paper bag under one arm. She opens her mouth to say something, then closes it. With her free hand, she pats my arm, then shuffles toward the stairs, waving at an imaginary cobweb as she passes through the pocket door into the rec room.

March 1945
Wetzlar, Germany

WHEN IRINA WAKES IN HER ROOM at Haus Friedwart, she realizes it is
Saturday. She is in no mood to spend the day by herself, staring into
the fields beyond the camp. She washes and dresses, resolved to find
something useful to do. When she walks into the kitchen, Frau Elsie
and Frau Lichen are preparing lunches for the children in the camp,
which Friedrich will deliver under one pretext or another. Irina falls in
with the women, placing thin pieces of cheese Frau Lichen has kept in
storage on the rye bread slices laid out on the counter. Frau Elsie looks
over at her and smiles but makes no comment, which Irina appreciates.

"Won't the guards notice?" Irina asks. With rationing as restric-
tive as it is, Irina finds it hard to believe any extra food will make it
through the gates.

"They have other things on their mind," Frau Elsie says, which
Irina takes as another sign that the Allies are near.

Restless, Irina decides to ride down to the camp with Friedrich.
They have just pulled up inside the gates when Olga, Viktor's girlfriend,

runs up to the car, her dark braids slapping her shoulders. Irina gets out to greet her.

"Sergei is back," Olga says, out of breath.

Irina feels the blood pounding in her ears. "Viktor?" she asks.

Olga shakes her head. She gives Irina's shoulder a gentle push and Irina begins to run to the other side of the camp. Sergei is standing in the middle of their room, glassy-eyed and unshaven, his clothes covered in dirt.

"It's very clean here," he says and pulls her to him.

June 2011
Niagara Falls, Canada

"FRAU ELSIE WAS BRAVE WOMAN," my grandmother says.

It is nearly eleven on Saturday morning. The house is calm and we wait in the living room. My grandmother has put on lipstick, a festive crimson, which sets off the brightness of her blouse. My mother has added a black wrap-around top to her black slacks. I wear an A-line light green floral sundress which I only now notice looks a lot like the couch's upholstery pattern.

"When American soldiers come to Wetzlar, Frau Elsie jump on my bicycle and ride down hill with white flag." My grandmother picks up a tumbler of water and takes a sip. "Yep," she says, "was bad war."

I wait for stories of exaltation, of victorious Americans riding in on their tanks, flags waving, women climbing the side of armoured vehicles. But these scenes do not come. In my grandmother's voice there is a flatness, as though the end of the war were only a brief marker between the end of one ordeal and the beginning of another.

"Sasha, open curtains," my grandmother says. "That way we see everyone when they come."

Dutifully, I push aside the lace so that we have an unobstructed view of the front lawn, the curb, the street, and the houses across the way.

"Pop always hated those curtains," my mother says absently.

"Yep, Pop like fresh air. Always happy outside. Pop good at being happy. Always singing something."

A silver town car pulls up in front of the house and slows beside the curb. My grandmother puts on her company face, a smoothing out of the anxieties around her eyes, the beginnings of a ready smile. There is a shuffle of shadows in the car, then Laurie and Jerry emerge. Even now, in their seventies, there is something of the golden couple about them as they make their way to the front door. It is only when they draw nearer that the years appear. Jerry places his hand gently against Laurie's back. He is still tall and blue-eyed and Laurie's curls are a little greyer but shining in the sun as she hurries up the driveway, adjusting her purse strap over the shoulder of her blouse.

"Here they are! Here they are!" my grandmother says, rising from the couch.

We meet on the doorstep and there are hellos and hugs. Laurie and my mother laugh, "If you hadn't moved so far, and for what? To be a hippie out there," Laurie says.

"I was never a hippie," my mother responds, and this is true, but now my grandmother clutches Laurie in her arms.

"Tyotya Ira," Laurie says, tears in her eyes.

"Hello, Irene," Jerry says and Laurie moves on to me, fond and knowing as she pats my arm. As we step back inside, two more cars drive up.

My uncle Alex, aunt Debi, and cousins appear, filling the house, pushing out the filmier presence of the morning, my cousins bringing Toronto with them, celebrity styles and sunglasses on their heads, all of us grinning, three through seven years old again.

My uncle says, "Coming through, coming through," a mid-sized cardboard box in his arms, taller than everyone, his silver head, as usual, travelling well ahead of the rest of his body. To my mother: "I got you this hot sauce. Wait 'til you try it. It will blow your head off!"

My eldest cousin's daughter, Madison, taller than last year, blonde like her father, with my cousin's face which is also my mother's, dodges through adult bodies to make sure my grandmother has added her grade-school picture to the little wooden table below the clock. Jerry helps my aunt with her jacket as they discuss wait times at the border crossings, and I notice she has changed her hair to a vivid copper pageboy.

My grandmother grasps my uncle's face in her cupped hands. When her hands fall from his cheeks he gives her a ziplock bag full of small black-and-white snapshots. "I've reorganized most of your photos by date," he says to her. "This bag is full of the early ones, forty-six to fifty-one."

After the initial press and glasses of lemonade, there is a scattering. My cousins head down to the rec room to reclaim past treasures and share them with Madison, and my aunt goes with them, her head bent to better hear Madison's chatter about swimming lessons. My mother, uncle, and Jerry head into the garden.

"Let's sit here where it's cool, Tyotya Ira," Laurie says to my grandmother and they claim a corner of the couch in the living room, their knees touching. My grandmother opens the bag of photos and both women pull out their reading glasses to look through the photographs.

"Here, see, your mother," my grandmother says. Perched on the arm of the sofa, I too look down at the photograph of Laurie's mother Milka, petite and laughing, squinting in the sun, holding a large, squirming baby.

"Who's the baby?" I ask.

"That Alex. Three months."

Laurie takes the photo from my grandmother, examines it and turns it over. In blue ink, in my grandmother's handwriting it reads, "Wiesbaden DP Camp, Germany, July, 1946."

"Your mother make those shorts she wearing herself, sewed them out of some material she trade for bread. So hot that summer, too hot to eat anyway, she say. Always so beautiful, your mother was, even in camp. Always look nice."

Even as my grandmother speaks, I feel it: the time that is missing, the months unaccounted for between the end of the war in the Leitz house and this sunny afternoon in a camp in Wiesbaden over a year later. There is nothing I can name, just a feeling of air on the platform, the warm, sulphurous draft, the train already out of sight.

My grandmother sighs. "Was hot that summer in DP camp but not when we arrive in April. So cold it was. Freezing. Amazing baby survive."

April 1946
Wiesbaden, Germany

THE DAMP FROM THE CEMENT FLOOR of the camp hallway works its way through the thin soles of Irina's shoes and creeps up the back of her legs. On either side of the hall, there are doors leading to tiny rooms. She takes this in, a corner of light, the smell of boiled cabbage. Sergei stands in front of her, his face grim. He is holding the two grey blankets given to them by the camp office.

"There are no rooms left," the official had said when they arrived at the front office. "You can sleep in the hall until someone leaves."

"But we have a baby . . ." Sergei said, pointing to Alex asleep in his carriage.

"Who doesn't?" the official shrugged wearily.

Irina wonders if they should have travelled further north to another DP camp, beyond the hundred-and-fifty kilometre train ride from Wetzlar. It has been six weeks since the baby was born, and Irina is still weak and anemic. All she wants is somewhere to lie down where the baby will be warm and dry. As Irina and Sergei stand there, a small, thin woman with a quick manner steps out of one of the rooms. She has a steel bucket in her hand, probably to get water from the communal pump. Her face is wide and curious as she stops to speak with them.

"Are you looking for your room?"

Sergei bites his lip so Irina answers.

"No, there is no room. We were told to sleep in the hall."

"With a baby?" the woman asks, her dark eyebrows shooting up in surprise.

Irina shrugs.

The woman seems to switch into high gear.

"No," she says decisively, "no, absolutely not. The baby will catch its death out here. You'll stay with us."

Irina is afraid that Sergei will protest, too proud to infringe on the small amount of space this woman has been given, but to her relief, he looks down at the baby carriage and says nothing.

"If you're sure?" Irina asks.

The woman has already taken hold of the carriage and pushes it down the hall with the bucket still in her hand.

"Of course," she says. "My name is Melania — Milka."

Milka angles the carriage to the right and wields it through an open door. Irina and Sergei follow, and Irina is dismayed. The room is the size of a small train compartment. There is a large man, dark-haired and powerful, with a thick moustache, sitting on a small stool in the corner. In front of him, two little girls play on a mattress with a tattered doll. The girls are about five and ten, the little one with blonde curls and the older one with auburn hair. The baby carriage alone probably takes up a sixth of the room when Milka parks it deftly in a corner.

"Can't leave it in the hallway. It will be gone by the morning. This is my husband, Panas, and the girls, Valya and Laura," she says. "These are . . ." She pauses and turns to them.

"Irina and Sergei . . . and Alexandre Nikifortchuk," Irina says, tripping on the last syllable. She slouches to make herself seem smaller.

"Irina and Sergei and Alex," Melania repeats. "They'll be staying with us for a while."

Irina waits for Panas's face to darken, to take his wife into the hall and ask her what she was thinking, but his face breaks into a wide grin. "Welcome to our palace," he says, with an expansive gesture around the room. When he rises from the stool, Irina realizes he is well over six feet. He steps over the mattress to shake their hands. "Valya, Laura, move over and make some room."

In the end, they stay with the Kantowskys for a month. Milka shames the office into giving them an extra mattress, and at night Irina, Sergei and Alex sleep at one end of the room while Panas, Milka, and the girls sleep at the other. There is only an arm's length between the families and at times Irina is tempted to extend her hand and smooth Laura's blonde curls from her flushed face as she sleeps.

During the day, Irina and Sergei resume their long walks in the fields beyond the camp, Alex small and drowsy on Sergei's shoulder. Laura tags along, becoming devoted to Sergei as he tells her stories of far-away kingdoms, monsters, princesses, and knights. One day when Milka is looking after Alex, the three of them are walking in the field when Laura begins pressing her small fists against Irina's thigh.

"You should go now," the little girl says gravely. "Sergei and I are going to get married, and I will own all of this." She waves her arm around the wide expanse of field, and then keeps spinning until she laughs and falls down. Sergei laughs, too, and lifts Laura onto his shoulders.

"Eto billo oujet davno, davno, billa malinkaya princessa svali Laura."

"Once, a very long time ago," Sergei begins, Laura's hands clutching his forehead, "there was a small princess named Laura."

As the weather warms, Sergei and Panas sit outside on benches in the evening, smoking and drinking bootlegged liquor. Sometimes Irina watches them play-boxing in the clay yard, or sitting at one of the few picnic tables, trying to wrestle plans from the little information available from the camp office. After Irina and Milka put the children to bed, they drink weak tea in mason jars, speaking quietly so that they don't wake the children.

When a room comes up, Irina, Sergei, and Alex move the baby carriage and their small suitcase down the hall, but they still see the Kantowskys every day. A few weeks later, Sergei and Panas are accepted together to work at a coal mine in Belgium. As a goodbye present to Alex, Sergei walks twenty kilometres to an American camp and trades what is left of his cigarettes for an orange. When he returns, he puts the orange, round and luminous, in the baby's hands. Now over a year old, Alex peers at the unfamiliar food before stuffing the whole thing in his mouth, peel and all.

Summer comes and the men leave for Belgium, promising to send for their families when they have made some money and found somewhere to live. Left on their own, Irina and Milka sneak over to the French side of the camp, fill gasoline containers with wine, summon up a careless look as they pass the guards, and sell the wine to other refugees. In this way, they can buy extra bread for the children and supplement their daily rations with black-market dry milk powder. They sew the little extra cash they have into the seams of their dresses, readying themselves for the moment they can join the men in Belgium.

Irina and Alex in Germany, 1947

June 2011
Niagara Falls, Canada

BY NOON, THE AROMA FROM THE oven draws everyone back to the main floor. My mother, cousins, and I ferry dishes from the kitchen to the table while my grandmother urges everyone to find a place to sit. "Time to eat! Time to eat!" she cries, waving her arms in small, circular motions as we squeeze around the table, everyone wedged in the space between the kitchen's pass-through window and the china cabinet, my grandmother, at the head, pushed almost into the living room by the table extension masked by the pink tablecloth with its lace overlay.

When the meat on sticks reach Jerry, his face softens. "Oh, Irene," he says. "You remembered."

"Yes, Jerry, I always remember your favourite," my grandmother says and Laurie laughs.

"That's why Jerry likes to come here," Laurie jokes. "All these foods, so much work! I never make them for you, do I, Jerry? Except the sausage, Tyotya Ira, we always make the sausage at Easter. It takes us two days, but it's worth it."

My uncle squeezes around the table, pouring out small glasses of champagne.

My cousins take up an off-kilter chorus of "Toast, Baba! Toast!"

My grandmother looks uncertain, then raises her glass.

"Happy everyone here," my grandmother says. She fidgets with the napkin in her lap, then raises her eyes. "When we get off boat in Halifax, we don't know what we come to. We take train, and all through Quebec we only see skinny cows. Such skinny cows! We think maybe this poor country. But we have good life here, good food. Kids grow. Pop and I very happy. Pop be very happy you all here today."

"Cheers," we all say. "To Pop," my mother adds.

There is the clink of glasses and cutlery and in the opening moments there is an elevated silence, the tenderness of the meat, the creamy filling of the potato vareniki, the acidic bite of the tomato sauce and cabbage. After a long minute, it is Laurie who breaks the silence.

"I remember the day you left Belgium, you know."

She turns to my uncle, who is salting his vareniki with a crystal shaker.

"You were always such a klutz! I was ten, you were five, and we had some money to buy candy. You tripped over my foot and broke your arm!"

"Was day we supposed to leave for Paris to take boat," my grandmother says, putting down her fork. "Lucky it was Thursday and Alex able to have cast put on right away. When Lucy born it was Sunday and all Belgian hospitals closed."

"Yes," Laurie says. "I remember. Mama told me to boil water."

"Pop find doctor, but the doctor drunk. Pop hold him by collar and say, 'You kill my wife and child, I kill you!'"

"But then Lucy was born and you and Mama pushed her all around town in the carriage with all the pink pillows," Laurie says.

My grandmother nods.

"Everyone look at Lucy in outfit I sew for her with all kind lace and say, 'La petite princesse!' We no speak much French, but Alex learn fast and talk to grocers in market. Only later we learn he buying imported Algerian cherry for all his friends —. put on our bill!

So expensive. I yell at grocer and at Alex and he say, 'But, Mama, imported cherries are better . . .'"

There is laughter at the table and my uncle shrugs.

"One day there was big explosion in coal mine where Panas and Pop working. Milka and I run to mine to see they still alive. Panas and Sergei okay, just covered in dust, but so many bodies come out of mine that day, that when we decide to leave."

"That's right," Laurie says, as though just remembering now.

"Of course that right," my grandmother says. "That the way it was."

After lunch, my cousins and I put the leftovers in Tupperware containers and fill the sink with soapy water. We snap wet tea towels at each other, sing Supremes songs into paper towel rolls that do little to absorb the sound. I gather up the plates from the dining room table. Most of the food has been demolished, though there is enough to feed twelve people again in the fridge downstairs. Only the lasagna is intact, barring a four-inch square in the right-hand corner of the pan. Two plates bear the marks of its burgundy sauce: a polite smudge on Jerry's plate and the outline of a modest, rectangular piece on my grandmother's.

In the late afternoon, the party drifts into the backyard, immune to the heat and humidity. Even my mother looks comfortable, as though our week here has reignited some latent, atavistic gene that reacclimatizes her to temperatures over thirty. My grandmother leads Jerry and Laurie on a tour of her garden, and they stop a moment to examine the tops of some tall poppies that are wilting in the sun. In the centre of the yard, my mother and cousins coach Madison on handstand technique, Madison's face flushed from the effort of throwing herself up against the crabapple tree in the middle of the lawn. My aunt, copper hair shining in the sun, is on her cell phone at the far end of the yard, looking at the neighbour's tomato plants. I sweat in one of the cushioned lawn chairs that surround the plastic patio set. My uncle sits across from me, Nikon around his neck, the cardboard box he was carrying earlier at his feet.

He has been fiddling with the settings on his camera, but now he reaches into the box, pulls out a small stack of photographs, sorts through them, and passes one to me. Even with mirrored sunglasses on, there is something about the set of his mouth, a blankness imposed against a smile that lets me know that whatever he is holding, it is the money shot.

I take the photograph, careful to touch only the rims with my fingers. I raise my own sunglasses and look carefully at the picture. The photograph is of three people: a couple with their backs turned, and a woman standing in front of a garden box. The image — *Someone was being artsy*, I think — is a black-and-white shot of me in my mid-twenties, with a slightly pronounced right incisor, the coltish look of one compelled by company but with half a mind to bolt, the waist-length dark hair, head tilted to the left in a perpetual pose that is the despair of my chiropractor. The sundress I am wearing is classically cut, bateau neckline, a style I favour. I have no memory of this scene.

My uncle is watching my face, though his own gives nothing away. I flip the photo. On the back, in my grandmother's handwriting, it says, "Fontaine l'Évêque, Belgium, 1947."

I look up at my uncle, who cannot contain himself. "It's you, isn't it?" He laughs. "But it's not you."

He glances at my grandmother, who is pinching the browned petals at the top of a poppy, throwing them to the wind.

"But I've seen photos of Baba when she was young," I say, a little churlish, a little unsettled by this trick of light or angles or whatever it is that is happening here. Unnerved, I search for differences and find them. My grandmother's forehead is broader, her eyes spaced further apart. Her torso is shorter than mine compared with the length of her legs. But there is no question we would be mistaken for each other in a crowd.

My uncle grins, a sardonic smile that says life is stranger and more uncertain than any of us care to admit. He leaves me with the photograph and wanders over to the rose bush, calling everyone over. The family sorts themselves into two lines and my uncle tries some test shots, adjusts the light exposure setting on the Nikon. My grandmother calls to me but for a long moment I sit there, listening to the sound the camera makes, the strange, condensed click of the shutter.

As afternoon becomes evening, we drift back into the house and then the house empties: first my cousins and Madison, then my uncle and aunt, who are visiting other relatives but will return the next day. By six o'clock, Jerry has the car keys in his hand, anxious about holiday traffic on the bridge.

"So good to see you all," Laurie says to us, folding her glasses and putting them in her purse. "Tyotya Ira, come down and stay with us some time."

"That would be nice, " my grandmother says. "Maybe some time."

"Goodbye, Irene," Jerry says. "It was a wonderful meal, truly."

"Thank you, Jerry. Drive safe, okay?"

Laurie is about to put down her purse and start talking again. Jerry puts his hand lightly on her elbow and nudges her toward the door.

"Let's go, Laurie. Time to go."

Laurie makes a motion to leave, then looks once more at my grandmother and her face goes blank, all the warmth and character stripped from its surface.

"You know what I remember?" she says. "I remember the last days in the work camp. The Americans were coming, we all knew they were coming, and one of the German commanders went crazy. He herded us to the far end of the camp with his gun, where there was a giant pit. I said to Mama, 'What is it?' And she says, 'It's a swimming pool. They're building a beautiful pool for us to go swimming in.' And when I looked down, there were already bodies in the pit, some of them still moving." Laurie's eyes refocus. "Another commander stopped the crazy one, took his gun away. But we were this close, you know? Sometimes I think about that."

An invisible cord seems to connect Laurie and my grandmother as they stand together in silence. It is my grandmother who breaks it.

"Take some food with you, Laura. Some meat on stick, vareniki . . ."

"No, no. I can't, Tyotya Ira. You're not supposed to take that stuff across the border and the guards with guns . . . I only come because I want to see you."

Laurie shakes her head and hugs my grandmother one last time, the animation coming back into her face.

"She had nightmares for years," Jerry says. He is standing next to me and says this in a low voice, the keys forgotten, suspended in his right hand. "For years she would wake up, screaming —"

"Goodbye, Tyotya Ira," Laurie says to my grandmother, gathering herself, taking my grandmother in her arms. "I'll see you soon."

Laurie and Jerry walk down the porch steps, down the driveway, arrange themselves in the car. Jerry beeps the horn gently. We stand on the porch and wave until the car is out of sight.

The three of us retreat into the living room and drop onto the couches. My grandmother leans against the arm of the couch, her lipstick smeared from the heat. She dabs at the corner of her mouth with a Kleenex, seemingly unfazed by Laurie's story.

"Was nice party," my grandmother says. "Very nice."

"It was good, Mom," my mother says, and I make a humming noise of agreement, still unnerved by the resemblance in the photo, at once revved and sleepy from the long afternoon.

My mother pauses a moment, gauging my grandmother's fatigue, but my grandmother is still bright with the success of the gathering.

"Family popravilisa a little, you notice? Everyone put on little bit weight —"

"Mom," my mother says, stopping my grandmother before she can run down the ways we all look a little meatier this year, though perhaps, I think, and noticing for the first time, this is because she herself has lost weight.

"Listen, Mom," my mother says, changing the subject. "Alex and I were talking. He and Debi are thinking about a trip to Ukraine and Russia. They would like you to go with them."

My grandmother stiffens her body against the sofa's back.

"No," she says finally. "I no think so."

"But you could see your sister." My grandmother's sister, Anya, is the only sibling my grandmother has been able to find. They speak occasionally on the phone when my grandmother can get past the drunken voice of Anya's husband.

My grandmother fidgets, smooths the crease in her slacks.

"I too old," she says at last.

"You're healthy," my mother says. "You could do it at your own pace."

My grandmother clearly considers another evasion but then changes course, squares her chin. There is a flash in her eyes.

"If I go, they no let me come back."

A dent forms on my mother's face, in the space between her eyebrows.

"Of course they would, Mom. You're a Canadian citizen now."

My grandmother's voice is flat. "They keep me there."

"Why would they do that?"

My grandmother's lips form a thin, tightly sealed line.

"Why, Mom?" The question is a chord. My mother is not just asking about this time. Other unanswered questions can be heard in her voice.

My grandmother sighs and looks out the window at the mellowing light of the suburban street.

"Doesn't matter now," she says.

"Mom," my mother says.

The challenge leaves my grandmother's face and she looks suddenly unsure, her eyes moving around the room. Finally, they settle on my mother's face. There is a shudder in my grandmother's body and for a moment I think this is where the truth will stay, locked inside her like a subterranean tremor.

"Tell me," my mother says.

My grandmother looks out the window again and I think, *That's it then. This is as far as this will go.* For a long moment my grandmother sits. But then something that to this day I cannot name overcomes her, whether it was the fading success of the party or some feeling of indebtedness to my mother for having helped bring it about. Or maybe she had just reached the end of whatever had kept her silent for so many years.

"After war," my grandmother speaks slowly and carefully, "Pop and I don't go to Soviet DP camp like we supposed to. When I leave Leitz house, we decide to hide in Polish DP camp. Think maybe we sent to Poland, we can travel back to village to find my family. Dangerous for us in Soviet section of camp. I tell you — how many times I tell you? — but you don't hear, not really. Pop was military during war. Russian soldier. His unit fell apart, everyone go everywhere. But Russians say Pop predatel."

She uses the Russian word for traitor. The word sits heavily in the room. I realize that in all the years of all the stories — of famine and Nazi round-ups and transport trains and Gestapo-policed work camps — I have never seen the scrambling anxiety that is in my grandmother's face now.

"Pop and I work for Germans in Leitz camp during war — no choice — but Russians again say we predatel, say we help the enemy. You no idea what that mean in Russia, to be predatel."

My grandmother looks up, unrelenting now.

"You want to know? What happen? The only reason we here is because we escape. You no idea what we do. To survive. Nice for some people: war ends, war over. But we have Communists after Nazis, and we never know when they come for us. Never."

I can see my mother take this in, pulling together years of fragmented stories and wary looks, abstract cautionary tales and strange, unexplained refusals.

"Was that why Pop watched those men, all those years ago, outside the house?"

"We don't know if they find us," my grandmother says. "We hear all kind things about secret police, how they find traitor after war, what they do to them." She shakes her head. "Maybe yes, maybe no. We don't know. No one know. We always look over shoulder."

"But Mom," my mother says, gently. "Mom . . . that was over sixty years ago."

My grandmother's eyes are dark, pitying our softness, our naivete.

"Sixty years not so long."

PART II

September 2011
Vancouver, Canada

I SIT AT MY ANTIQUE WRITING DESK, which is battered and slim-legged, in a far recess of the apartment living room. The walls are yellow and the autumn sun filters through the lace curtains. I rearrange my books and papers and push the printer on the floor over to the left to make space for an infant bouncy seat, newly acquired.

I turn on the laptop, find the Word file that auto-saved on July 5 as MEATONSTICK. It is a record of our summer visit to Niagara Falls: notes on Elsie Kühn-Leitz and transcriptions of conversations with my grandmother. I have spent the summer working on my Mina Loy research, gathering the pieces of her story, the Florentine villa where she visited Gertrude Stein, the New York neighbourhood where she scoured the streets for objects she would later turn into radical collage. But it is the gaps in my grandmother's file that have preoccupied me through an island summer of note-taking and beach wading, absence that plays on my mind even as the baby grows firm.

Many of these silences I cannot fill: the things my grandmother will not say, the sparsity of English-language sources that mention Elsie Kühn-Leitz. Where there is abundance is in archival footage — reel after reel of the Allies entering camps at the end of the war. Some of these films have the propaganda feel of the liberating army. More often they are documentary, visual evidence of scenes no one could adequately describe.

One of the films from this period, *Le retour*, was made by the French photographer Henri Cartier-Bresson, that sometimes visitor to Haus Friedwart, the same man who pioneered street photography outside Parisian cafés throughout the 1920s. During the war, Cartier-Bresson was himself a POW and forced labourer in Germany for almost three years before he escaped. *Le retour* was commissioned by the United States Office of War Information in 1945. It traces the journey of forced labourers and other displaced persons on their way home at the war's end, standing in line, shuffling onto trains, meeting jubilant relatives in the Gare d'Orsay. While in a DP camp in Dessau, Cartier-Bresson filmed a former prisoner in the moment she recognized the Belgian woman who denounced her to the Nazis. He left the movie camera running to also capture the scene with his Leica. In the film as in the stills, we see the woman strike her denouncer across the face. Behind them, a group of refugees watches impassively.

Not all post-war returns were the same, as the books on my desk make clear. The terms of the Yalta agreement, signed by Churchill, Roosevelt, and Stalin in February of 1945, divided the soon-to-be-conquered Germany into four occupied zones controlled by the British, Americans, Soviets, and French. Article 1 under repatriation saw civilian deportees handed over to troops from their homeland. In practice, this meant that Yugoslavian and Soviet civilians were often repatriated without their consent. Most Eastern workers who were returned to the U.S.S.R. were, at the very least, interrogated and ostracized. Many more were sent to still another forced labour camp, this time on home soil. Some women returned with children born to them of rape while in Germany. Others returned empty-handed, their babies taken at Nazi birthing facilities. Some labourers disappeared during the journey home from Germany under Russian guard. At the war's end, there was no monopoly on suffering. But my grandparents were right to be afraid.

Next to my books and notes sits a slim stack of 2x3 inch photographs with thin white borders and scalloped edges. They are photographs of my grandparents' first few months in Canada. Many of these photographs are taken at Niagara Falls and some have Pyoter and Katya Korban in them, the couple who sponsored my grandparents' move to Canada. The men wear fedoras and trench coats. The women are neat in church dresses and hats. My mother is a baby and my uncle has the cocksure smile of the kindergarten clown. His look defines the photographs, making the lines on Pyoter Korban's face look more severe and Katya Korban seem all the more ethereal and withdrawn. My grandparents look stunned, like people waking from the long night.

I reach for my phone and check the time difference on the clock radio. Nine a.m. here. Noon in Niagara Falls. My grandmother will be home in the hour before her first soap opera. As the phone rings, I rehearse. Please tell me what happened, I will say. Tell me what happened in the Polish DP camp. Even in the coolness of the coastal morning, my palm feels damp against the receiver as I wait for my grandmother to answer.

Spring 1945
Wetzlar, Germany

WHEN THE BOMBING ENDS, THE AMERICANS saunter into Wetzlar with guns slung loosely at their sides. The German guards are long gone. The Leitz Werke labourers are left prisoners with no one imprisoning them, prisoners who do not leave their prison. There are rumours that on arrival, ninety American soldiers walked into the Leitz factory, each exiting with a new model Leica around his neck.

In the house, Frau Elsie offers Irina continued employment. It is tempting to stay, but in the end, Irina and Sergei decide they will return east to find Irina's family. In the DP camps that are established in the city's abandoned army barracks, there are still more rumours: rumours of how the Russians took their revenge on the German population as they swept west, rumours about what they intend to do with Soviet citizens who worked for the enemy. With limited options, Irina and Sergei decide to register as Polish, from the part of Poland that has not been given over to Stalin as a spoil of war, the part that is relatively free.

In the incongruous geography of the war's end, the Polish DP camp borders the American base camp. In the evenings, Irina can hear the laughing voices next door. Irina grasps the sound if not the meaning of new words: *beat-'em-good, goddamn-krauts*. Less frequently, she overhears more sombre phrases that let her know the Americans, too, are thinking of Poland. "Auschwitz," "Belzec," "Treblinka."

As the days go on, Sergei makes friends with the American soldiers, his easy manner gliding through the language barrier. The Americans sell Sergei their cigarettes that he in turn peddles on the black market in the surrounding towns to make extra money for food. Irina helps Sergei pack an old suitcase they find abandoned by the side of the road. They pack the stiff, weather- beaten case with row on row of small red boxes with a white coat of arms, lions on either side, a knight's helmet on top. "Pall Mall" are the first English words Irina learns to read.

Again abetted by her German, Irina finds work in the Polish camp office. The director is also Ukrainian passing as Polish, a short, bald man with a squint that emerges when confronted with stories of rheumatic fever outbreaks, depression, and suicide among the survivors. A British administrative assistant named Tamara, friendly, dark-haired, and freckled, gives Irina a British women's auxiliary uniform so that she can pass more easily through different sections of the camp. The uniform is olive and worn with a beige blouse. The skirt is knee-length and the jacket has brass buttons and three lines like ascending arrow tips embroidered on the upper sleeves. Food in the camp is limited, but there is cabbage. It is Tamara who teaches Irina to make cabbage rolls, something she herself has learned from the Polish women, how to tightly wind the rice and tomato sauce in the boiled green leaves.

For eight weeks, Irina and Sergei live in the Polish camp, waiting for the moment they can leave. When the Russian trucks roll in, it is a surprise. The Russians have a base camp in Turnhout, more than 300 kilometres away. The raids have mostly been farther north. There are reports that conditions for DPs at the Turnhout camp are worse than they were under the Nazis: dirtier, food riddled with bugs, a new level of violence.

The Russian commander who walks into the office is tall, like Irina's father, but short-haired and slack-jawed with deep creases on either side of his nose. The commander walks over to the director's desk, snorts derisively, and with feigned formality, places a list on the director's desk.

"A copy for you, Comrade, since your name is on it."

Once again Irina finds herself on a list, this time among the sixty Russians and Ukrainians known to be hiding in the Polish camp, traced through the Reich's immaculate records. The list is accompanied by a set of identity photographs and Sergei is there too. The Russians identify the fugitives in the bright grey light of the German spring, then give their prisoners ten minutes to gather a few things. Sergei takes his extra shirt, his shaving brush, his razor. In her canvas drawstring bag, Irina packs the dresses from Frau Elsie, a bar of soap she has managed to stow away. The perfume bottle she tucks into the pocket of the women's auxiliary uniform. Bags in hand, Sergei and Irina join the others in the central assembly yard. The commander stands on the back of a truck and speaks loudly to the crowd.

"While in Germany you have worked for the enemy against the Soviet Union and then attempted to escape. You have therefore been identified as collaborators. You will be taken to Siberia to work in corrective labour camps. Those who resist will be shot."

The commander rests his hand on his holster. The prisoners are silent. Irina wonders if someone will step forward, be killed now rather than over years of grinding labour in the gold mines of Siberia, but no one moves.

The soldiers push the prisoners into cargo trucks, packed shoulder to shoulder, back to front. Pressed against Sergei, Irina wants to take his hand but cannot. "Irina," he whispers in her ear. "Irina." Irina knows what he is thinking. That they must find some way out. That the alternative is intolerable. But it is impossible to find words for an escape that is nowhere in sight.

When they reach the Russian camp six hours later, the men and women are separated and sent to dormitories at opposite ends of the camp, their hair smelling of fuel fumes. Irina is forced into a room with twenty other women and children. They sleep on wooden benches or on the floor on dirty blankets abandoned by the Germans. That night, Irina stares at the wall. She thinks about her room at Haus Friedwart, the light from the garden, the noise in the kitchen as the day began. *How foolish*, Irina thinks, her face pressed against the wooden bench. *How foolish to think this war was over.*

September 2011
Vancouver, Canada

JOHN AND I LOLL ON THE couch as the light darkens against the yellow wall. Our baby, Tatianna, naps in the paler yellow of her chair. We sit there, trying to figure out the BabyBjörn my parents bought us. It has two parts: the harness itself, designed to hold the baby, and the straps that crisscross around the wearer's back and circle around the waist. All of the buckles are colour coded to be completely idiot-proof. We are clearly below the curve. We fiddle and curse, thwarted by the plastic mechanisms that hold the two parts together. John, earnest about this kind of problem-solving, and believing there is a solution, bends his neck in concentration. His broad, determined face has lost its customary geniality and is twisted by the complexity of what ought to be the easiest of tasks.

Sensing John's commitment to the cause, I browse the advertising insert instead. All of the Björn parents are Euro-sleek models. The men have long, symmetrically cut hair, pointy shoes, aquiline noses. The Björns are colour coded to match their outfits: canary yellow, cerulean blue, forest green. The women look eighteen. Something about their perfect coiffure gives the whole thing the air of the ridiculous. I am high on our own ineptitude, on our outrageous luck. I look over at John, who continues to fiddle with the buckles and the harness around his shoulders.

"What does Bruce Springsteen sing to his children?"

John looks up from the harness.

"'Björn in the USA'!"

John sighs, but I haven't slept in three nights.

"What do you call a baby who converts?"

"Please don't."

"Björn again!"

And we are laughing, a bit stupid, a bit manic after the last few days, the hospital, the machines, the fluorescent lights. This small, wild figure who changes everything.

May 1945
Turnhout, Belgium

THE FIRST MORNING IN THE RUSSIAN camp at Turnhout, Irina is given
a pass to buy bread in the British section of the camp. The Russian
soldiers allow her through with a warning that she needs to be back
by ten.

"Of course she'll be back," one of the soldiers says to the other,
making a lewd gesture with his tongue. "How can she resist me?"

The men laugh, and Irina feels a chill. She has slept in the auxiliary uniform. The prisoners have not had access to showers. She feels
gritty and soiled but she knows that for the soldiers that is hardly the
point. She hurries on, the pass pressed against her thigh.

The British zone of the Turnhout camp is full of assorted trucks and
soldiers. Irina recognizes the British, Russian, and American uniforms
from her work in the Polish camp. The soldiers mill around, intermixed
with the displaced who are equally recognizable in their mishmash of
clothing: black-and-white striped prisoner garb, army jackets, civilian
pants. Irina looks for a line. Lines are always where the bread is. Even

in Stanytsia, Irina would stand for hours at the Collective bakery only to be told there was nothing left. Seeing a raggedy snake's tail of refugees in the distance, she heads in that direction, dodging a group of American soldiers drunk in the morning.

Irina is close to reaching the line when she feels a hand on her arm. Her instinct is to pull back but she is careful about lowering her arm slowly to her side.

"Excuse me, miss," a British soldier says to her in English. He is one of the palest people Irina has ever seen, with light blue eyes and hair so blonde it is almost white. His smile reminds Irina of Sergei's, easy and charming. Irina has the impression he is the type of man who makes a habit of chatting with women, but he is also a soldier, and so she stops.

"I'm sorry," she says in German. "I don't speak English."

"But you're wearing a British uniform?" he asks, switching easily to German.

"My friend gave it to me," Irina says and then, feeling this needs more explanation, "I am — I was one of the Eastern workers."

"Right," he says, unperturbed. "Where are you off to?"

"I am going to buy bread," Irina says, keeping her tone neutral.

"No. Where next?"

"The Soviet Union." She answers him seriously though he is treating the conversation lightly. "The Russian soldiers are making us go back."

The soldier straightens. Irina looks more carefully at the epaulettes on his uniform and realizes he is a lieutenant.

"Do you know what is happening to those who return?" He enunciates carefully, to make sure she is following. "Stalin is treating everyone who worked in Germany as a traitor. He is killing them." He slices his finger across his throat to make sure she understands. "And it's bloody frustrating to liberate people just to see them killed."

"We were told work camps . . ."

"It's a lie to get you away from the international camps. We've already had reports of truckloads of dead Soviets."

Irina searches but she can't find words, not in any language.

"Listen," the lieutenant says urgently. "My unit is leaving the camp. You're dressed in British uniform."

"My husband . . ."

Having suggested the plan, he does not pull back. "Get him. Meet the truck in section two."

Irina walks quickly back through the camp, past the tents and flimsily constructed wooden structures that have risen out of the dust. When she reaches the Russian section she slows and tries to catch her breath. She feels bile collecting at the back of her throat when she sees the Russian soldier who harassed her earlier.

"Back already?"

"The line is very long. My husband and I will have to take turns."

The soldier seems bored of playing with her.

"Fine. Still ten for your return."

Irina walks quickly to the men's quarters, peering into the stall-like rooms until she finds Sergei. Irina pulls him into the hall, whispers in his ear. Sergei's jaw clenches. He ducks back into the room for his shoes. He and Irina hurry across the camp, keeping their hands low at their sides as the Russian guards wave them through.

In section two, they find the British army truck. A dozen British soldiers are stowing their supplies and hefting canvas hold-alls into the back. The pale-faced lieutenant looks around and beckons to Sergei. Sergei hesitates then follows as the lieutenant points to a corner of the truck bed, where Sergei folds himself into a ball. One of the soldiers throws a khaki-coloured blanket over his body. "Let's go," the lieutenant says. The men pile into the truck. The lieutenant helps Irina into the back and stands beside her and throws an arm around her shoulders. Irina stares at the blanket. The soldiers' lace-up boots are inches from Sergei's body. The truck lurches and begins rolling toward the edge of the camp. Irina tries to relax her hands, to hold them loosely at her sides, as though she is part of the women's auxiliary, tired but happy to be going home at last. At the checkpoint, the truck idles and Irina hears Russian voices.

A Russian sentry climbs up into the truck.

"It has been reported there are Soviets in this truck," he says in English and then Russian. Irina is frozen, knowing it is over, that someone — who? — has seen them and given them away.

The British lieutenant does not change expression. He gestures toward his unit, looks annoyed by the inconvenience, keeps the arm casually around Irina's shoulders. "We're all English here."

The men in the lieutenant's unit shuffle and make off-hand, angry comments. The Russian peers into the truck, scans the uniforms, slows as his eyes reach Irina.

"We're all English," the lieutenant repeats. He makes steady, unwavering eye contact with the Russian. There is a tightening of the air. The sentry takes a step forward, but a fellow soldier calls to him from outside the truck. With a sharp, sudden movement, the Russian turns and jumps back down to the ground. After a moment, the truck rocks forward.

The British soldiers take Irina and Sergei as far as the Turnhout train station. The lieutenant starts a collection among the men and hands Sergei some money. He wishes them luck with a touch of his cap, then jumps back in the truck. Irina and Sergei stand outside the station, watching the dust clouds rise as the truck drives away.

"And that how we escape, Sasha," my grandmother says over the phone. This breakthrough comes about quite casually one day when the baby is three months old.

"And this was May of 1945?"

"Ya, May."

"But you didn't meet the Kantowskys in the camp in Wiesbaden until the spring of 1946?"

There is silence on the line.

"Baby. Tell me how is baby. Tatianna is okay?"

Fall 2011
Vancouver, Canada

FOR A LONG TIME, I DO not get any further in my grandmother's story. The train station in Turnhout is as far as she will go. The baby is small and warm and immediate as skin. When I do go back to the file, it is to fill in details. My grandmother remembers the kindness of the German staff at Haus Friedwart, how close they were with the family — but not their names. Frau Elsie gave my grandmother a small closet full of clothes, but what items? The grey dress. She remembers the grey dress.

For every detail that remains obscure, there is a day my grandmother recalls with forensic clarity. The day Elsie Kühn-Leitz was taken by the Gestapo and the day she returned to the house are two such days. And so I return to questions I have been asking since the summer, questions about what could have happened to Elsie Kühn-Leitz in the Gestapo jail to make a woman like that crawl up the staircase of her own home on her hands and knees. The few books about Elsie Kühn-Leitz are mostly German-language collections compiled by her family: her son, Knut Kühn-Leitz, and her son-in-law, Cornelia's husband, Klaus Otto

Nass. The Nass book contains a complete version of Elsie Kühn-Leitz's autobiographical essay. After some time, I have the essay translated by a very bright German-born doctoral student named Kerstin. When we meet, I ask Kerstin for her impressions. Not so much of events as of the writer. Elsie Kühn-Leitz, seen from another angle.

Kerstin considers this question, turns it over, the fluorescent lights of the university office hitting the red highlights in her hair, the bronze rims of her glasses. She looks like someone doing the math to balance a complicated equation. When she speaks it is slowly, thoughtfully, as though transferring the equation to paper.

"Obviously she was a very brave woman," Kerstin says. "There's no denying that. But the words she uses sometimes in the essay — well, it's clear she was of her class and of her time. You notice when she talks about giving the blue blouse to Maria Holliwata, how she says the Eastern women love to 'strut around in colourful clothes.' And also in the jail, the way she refers to the women who are prostitutes as 'Hamburg and Berlin types.' They're not big things. But we are all marked by our class and our time."

There are accounts about Elsie Kühn-Leitz in English, mainly written for children. In these books, as in my grandmother's stories, she is the heroine. These stories are about bravery in difficult times. There are no blue blouses, no women from Hamburg or Berlin. But they are vivid accounts told in 14-point type, written for the intermediate-level reader. They contain photographs of Elsie, her father, and the children.

When I read Kerstin's translation, the focus sharpens. The labour camp and the Frankfurt jail come into fuller view. Mostly, Elsie Kühn-Leitz's essay is a dispassionate cataloguing of the events of the fall of 1943. But she begins with a pensive, retrospective passage:

Wetzlar, Germany

January 1947

It has been over three years since I was released from the Gestapo Prison in Frankfurt/Main. No doubt this is an account I should have written immediately after my release. But once a person has been in contact with the Gestapo, surveillance is ongoing. The house could have been searched at any time and a written account of my prison experience could have led to rearrest. One does not leave invitations of this kind lying around for the Gestapo.

In any event, the passage of time is healing for those who have been marked in body and soul. Time is coupled with forgetting. But complete forgetting is impossible for those who have suffered so much. They carry a "mental birthmark" that can never be erased. To go back to a time of such difficulty, when all life was in danger of being suffocated, is in itself a kind of suffocation. But not to write down an account of this time is equally a suffocation of truth.

From here, not unlike my grandmother, Elsie Kühn-Leitz mixes the said with the unsaid, the glacier's tip with the mass beneath the waterline. For all my plans to maintain a distance from this essay, I slip. Everything I have seen, heard, and read coalesces in a series of images drawn from black-and-white footage that now fills my mind late in the flattened night, shot through by the cry of the baby. I begin to think in vivid, visual terms about the woman who lay on a folding prison bed on a September night, a night that feels in no way distant.

September 1943
Frankfurt, Germany

ELSIE LIES ON THE FOLDING BED, listening to the bugs travel through the wood-chip stuffed mattress. She cannot see in the darkness, but she has already memorized the contents of the cell: the folding table, the shelf, the bucket, the metal door. When the kalfaktoren come, it is early and with breakfast trays, a piece of dark bread, a cup of metallic water. Then there is work duty, but in the first week Elsie is left in her cell while others report to the kitchen, the cleaning station, the sewing room, assignments called out by the guards. Mid-morning there is exercise, where the women shuffle around a sandy track. Then a return to the cells, followed by an afternoon work period. All day, throughout the day, women are escorted by female guards to the interrogation rooms. The names of the interrogators are whispered among the women: Albrecht, Wolff, Thorn, Gabusch, Jager. The women call the interrogation rooms the kitchens.

Dinner comes, usually another piece of black bread and a root vegetable soup. Elsie estimates her intake at seven hundred calories a day, enough to survive, but just. She wonders if someone, anyone, is pressing to have conditions improved for the prisoners. But as the days blur she begins to doubt that any outside influence could penetrate. The thick walls of her cell, the regulation of every movement, the absence of choice, the bending of will. She begins to believe the jail's boiler, with its groans and murmurs, is some essential organ in a vast, unfeeling body.

The nights are more varied. The female guards pass through infrequently, often only to escort an inmate to nighttime interrogation. In this moment the footsteps pass there is silence, a willing of strength among the prisoners for the woman walking numbly or wild-eyed down the aisle, a woman who looks so very much like themselves.

Without the guards, the women are less intent on being as unremarkable as possible and break the silence imposed on them during the day. Elsie comes to recognize the full-bodied vocal tones of the woman in the cell on her right, whom she cannot see through the wall that separates them but who recites passages from the Bible into the night: "We are afflicted in every way, but not crushed; perplexed, but not driven to despair; persecuted, but not forsaken; struck down, but not destroyed."

Down the hall, a fortune teller calls out her own prayers, to heathen gods, to the force of her own clairvoyance, until the women near her jeer or beg her to stop. The second night, Elsie listens to the sound of a woman trying to muffle her tears with some piece of material, the grey blanket, probably, in the cell to her left. Elsie herself tries to breathe through the stench from the buckets, in for two, out for three, pressing her lungs against the fear-constricted muscles of her chest. She listens to the woman crying, the rasp of her own body, the hum and bang of the boiler, the orchestral decrepitude of Klapperfeldstrasse 5.

It is not until the third day, in a moment where the heavy doors are open so the prisoners can dump their buckets in the basement bathrooms, bringing washing water back in the same, that Elsie notices the young woman in the cell across from her. At first, Elsie believes she is quite mad, a dark pixie, thin body taut and straight, ignoring the actions of her cellmates and moving through a series of condensed motions, a slight dart forward, swaying slightly back, her eyes elsewhere. Pushing her mind beyond the incongruity of the scene, Elsie recognizes the movements and tone of Odette's entrance in *Swan Lake*. Watching the young woman's port de bras through the space between the doors, Elsie is transported to the balconies and frescoed dome of the Staatsoper Stuttgart. It is only when the young woman lowers her arms and returns to herself, smiling slightly, that Elsie again feels the press of her own confinement.

The fourth night, Elsie hears a buzzing noise which at first seems like just another layer of prison sound. But then the woman in the cell beside her cries "bomb!" and there are screams and the scurry of rats and women. When the bomb lands, it deafens Elsie to all other noise. With nowhere to go, Elsie shelters in a far corner of the cell, pressing herself against the cinderblock she knows may fall in and crush her. There is another wave of sound, a shudder through the building, dust and ceiling plaster that fall like rice at a wedding. The voice in Elsie's mind repeats one word over and over: *Trapped*.

When the bombing is over, Miss Heldig, the blonde guard, walks down the aisle, banging her billy stick against the metal doors, yelling, "Get up! Get up off the floor, you vermin! Back to your beds!" The woman next door is now hyperventilating, and Elsie hears a groaning series of breaths, a choking reflex. Legs numb with shock, Elsie crawls to her cot, onto the mattress, under the grey blanket. She feels some primal function inside her flip a switch. For the first time in four nights, she sleeps.

The next morning, Elsie is disoriented and slow. She is paired for morning exercise with a distinguished woman in her sixties, her erect posture clashing with the slouching material of her dress. When she speaks, Elsie recognizes the clear clipped consonants and mellifluous Bavarian tones of the woman in the cell on her right, the one who nightly speaks out a prayer of encouragement to those in the cells around her.

"The Baroness Thusnelda, my dear," she says quietly to Elsie as they make their way out to the overcast light of the yard. "Elsie Leitz, yes? A pleasure to know you."

For the first time since her arrival in prison, Elsie feels something other than shock or terror. The baroness clutches at her collar as though it were a fine silk scarf, introduces herself as though she were receiving guests in her drawing room. Dimly, Elsie begins to appreciate the baroness's manipulation of circumstances, and as this understanding settles over her, the baroness gives her a wry, appreciative glance.

The baroness is quiet as they pass a guard and step over the threshold into the yard, but then begins a muted, forbidden commentary. Elsie keeps her head down, watching the dust-covered shoes of the prisoners in front of her. Maintaining the air of a gossipy social visit, the baroness also tucks her head, speaking to Elsie out of the corner of her mouth.

"The wardens choose the female guards for their attractiveness."

Elsie hesitates.

"They are prisoners themselves — or they were, at the women's correctional facility across the road — before they came here. They don't want to be sent back to jail and the wardens know how to use that in all sorts of ways, none of them good for us."

"Silence!" yells Miss Heldig, the guard nearest to them. For the first time, Elsie sees more than the grey uniform and realizes the guard is a very comely young woman in her early twenties, her thick blonde hair pulled back in a low bun.

The baroness looks pointedly at Elsie, then assumes a blank expression as they pass the guard.

"Do you see that woman over there, the one with the birthmark on her neck?" Elsie's new friend murmurs, gesturing with a tilt of her head.

Elsie carefully glances across the yard. The woman with a cloud-shaped birthmark is young and pale.

"She's here because she told a joke at a party, turned a picture of Hitler around saying he would take the food away if he knew how good it was." The baroness turns her head slightly to indicate the woman's walking partner. "The woman next to her, the heavier one, has five children. She was arrested because she did laundry for a Lithuanian man, baked him a cake, and gave him some cigarettes on his birthday."

"What about her?" Elsie asks, gesturing to the young dancer now making her way around the track behind the laundress.

"Isabella. Elegant, isn't she? She's a Russian aristocrat who came as a child after the Revolution. She speaks several languages, so the Nazis think she might be a spy." The baroness catches Elsie's eye again then slides her glance down the line to the women behind Isabella. Even without their makeup, there is something about the way the women hold themselves that leads Elsie to believe they are Hamburg and Berlin types.

"Arrested for hanging out with questionable characters," Thusnelda confirms. "Prison is a great leveller, I'll give you that much. Take the woman passing the doorway, now. The short, hefty one with the clenched jaw."

Elsie looks over to see a truculent woman with an aggressive stride bumping up on the heels of the woman in front of her.

"That's Kathe. She was a railway guard, arrested for being a communist, part of some radical organization. Watch out for her — she'll find out who you are, eventually, and she brought all of her class prejudice to jail with her . . ." The baroness cocks her head like a curious bird taking in the scene. "It's a funny sort of garden party."

Elsie feels her curiosity shift to the woman beside her.

"What about you? What have you been charged with?"

"My dear, what a quaint idea." Thusnelda almost laughs but then flattens her expression as the guard turns in their direction. They walk along in silence for a moment until they round the bend and are sheltered from the guard's view by the women in front of them. "I've been charged with nothing. I am merely an annoying old woman who told a joke about Goebbels to the wrong person."

Without turning her head, her eyes turn sharply toward Elsie. "If you are going to make it in here, you'll need to let that go, the idea of any kind of justice. That could drive you crazy, it really could."

Elsie realizes that she has assumed some kind of formal charges, however trumped up, would be brought against her. That there would be a trial, if only in a kangaroo court. She had not considered the possibility of indefinite limbo, and she suddenly feels that the prison is an abyss from which she will never emerge. Her sense of freefall is interrupted by a halt in the line and the sickening sound of something hard repeatedly striking something resonant and human.

The double line of prisoners clears to reveal the blonde guard, Miss Heldig, striking one of the Hamburg women with her billy stick, her shoulders rising and falling in muscular rhythm. The screams of the woman on the ground are blunted by the inanimate forms of the prisoners around her, the blood streaming from between her teeth all the more gruesome for its bright colour in a landscape of stone and grey.

Elsie feels the dry bread from breakfast rise in her throat, but her companion looks on as though the vicious attack is a regular part of the routine. The guard gives the sobbing woman on the ground a final kick in the stomach before ordering her walking-mate to clean her up in the lavatory.

"The guards had their training for beastliness this morning," the baroness says, as though by explanation.

"Their what?"

"The Gestapo officers come in once a week. Special training ordered by Himmler to rile up the female guards. It's a clever system, when you think about it."

"But what did she do?"

"The woman was a prostitute in Hamburg. After today's 'training' that no doubt cuts close to the bone. It's a clever system, as I say."

The walking begins again, and Elsie falls mechanically into line. The baroness straightens her spine and walks on, holding tightly to a life no longer hers. As they are filtered into the dimness of the prison, Thusnelda is pulled ahead by the stream of women, and Elsie watches her back recede, her carriage straight in the shuffling crowd.

That night, lying on her cot, Elsie is again engulfed by the unreality of this universe over which she has no control. She listens to the wailing of the fortune teller down the hall. There are shouts from some of the women, the sound of something hard being hurled against a metal door in a frustrated bid for quiet. Against the backdrop of the woman's ravings, Elsie thinks about betrayal. About the informers who turned in so many of these women to gain some advantage. About Frau Gerke, the woman who gave up Elsie's own name under torture and continues to denounce her with venemous accusations of coercion. About Maria, who so often leaned laughingly against her desk in the work camp. About Maria whom she never suspected, not once.

When the guards rouse the prisoners at four the next morning, Elsie has barely slept. And so, for a moment, she wonders if she isn't hallucinating when, as the women are being assembled for work duty, the fortune teller and the two Hamburg women are hustled down the hall by the guards, the fortune teller screaming along the way. The two Hamburg women are expressionless, the one who endured yesterday's beating staring wearily out from under the scabs and bruises covering the left side of her face.

"Where did they take them?" Elsie is able to slide her way over to the baroness as the line begins to move toward the workrooms.

The baroness observes her steadily for a moment.

"Auschwitz," she says at last. "They took them to Auschwitz."

Winter 2011
Vancouver, Canada

THAT WINTER, I AM FORTUNATE TO be on maternity leave. This gives me time with the baby but also time to continue tracing the past.

For all of that, much of the year is not spent inside but out, walking a stroller circuit of Denman, Robson, Davie, and Burrard, the four major streets that frame our leafy residential neighbourhood. The stroller, too, is yellow, with a large undercarriage I chose especially for groceries. The No Frills at the corner of Nelson and Denman is often our last stop on the way home, where I pick up canned goods and the good German rye. The interior of the store, as anyone who shops there will tell you, is painted an aggressive shade of fluorescent banana peel, designed to reinforce the idea that little has been spent on extras like designer paint. Combined with the unusual amount of sun we have had through the winter months, it is a very yellow year.

Of all the intersections we pass through on these walks, Denman and Davie is the most scenic, opening up as it does on the panorama of English Bay, the maple-lined seawall to Second Beach, and the broad expanse of Stanley Park. To the east runs the path to the bridges and the small ferry landing to Granville Island. The bike lane that runs behind this path, beside Beach Avenue, is lined with palm trees. Each of these palms is like a thin, hairy thumb pressed against the nose of the rest of the country, a blatant, imported symbol of February patio dining and March cherry blossoms. More than this even, it is an assurance to all who have travelled far that this is the spot, the land of milk and honey. The colour palette of the corner is further proof of this exceptionalism — the yellow leaves and pink skies of autumn, the whitecaps against the orange hulls of the freighters, the graduating blues of sky, mountains, and water. And always there is the sound of the ocean rolling over the beach, the coastal lullaby that murmurs indefinably of the land's end and new beginnings.

In the end, the year divides itself not so much in seasons as segments: there are the days with the baby, the landscape of our walks, the essence of this time, the centre of what I remember. But during Tatianna's afternoon naps, three hours like some kind of mid-day night, I immerse myself in the reconstruction of two distinct periods: May 1945 to April of 1946, the centrepiece of my grandmother's missing year, and September to late November of 1943, the three months Elsie Kühn-Leitz spent in the Gestapo jail. It would be pointless to maintain that I experienced these moments as separate from each other just as it would be untrue to say that the year as a whole wasn't underpinned by a profound lack of sleep, which gives everything about it a strangely vivid quality. At the same time, that vividness does not make it linear. That year and the year after were lived in fragments, in snapshots of time and snatches of sleep. Piecing it together is an act of radical collage.

On weekends, John walks with us, and we follow the seawall to the playground at Second Beach. Here, along with all the other parents, we succumb to the photo op: bundled kids in their playsuits, yellow tube-slide, red fire truck, iPhone cornucopia. The Björn sits solidly across John's shoulders, but we struggle with it, still. One day a woman standing outside the liquor store on Davie takes pity on us. While I hold the baby, the woman, with grey-blonde hair and a wide, patient face, shows us how the straps go, over and around, over and around, her hands moving deftly around John's waist, the buckles coming together, the satisfying sound of the click. The woman smiles at us, tells us she has three kids, all grown. But some things you never forget.

Walk to Stanley Park:
John and Tatianna, 2012

I talk with my grandmother on Sundays. She is distant during these phone calls. It is only in talking with my mother that I learn what is troubling her, a series of incidents, not significant in themselves until they are: a forgotten doctor's appointment, the stove left on. One day she drives the Oldsmobile to Zehrs and can't remember how to get home. Conversations begin about what to do, calls between my mother on the island and my uncle in Lewiston, calls between the island and me in Vancouver, calls across the country to Niagara Falls. Home care is brought in, a family visiting schedule established. It is suggested my grandmother could come to Vancouver, but there are gaps — the three months' wait to be eligible for healthcare after the move, the insurance benefits from my grandfather's pension plan at the Norton Factory that will not follow her out of province. My grandmother herself is adamant about not leaving her house: "When I dead you put me wherever you want. Until then, I stay here."

In the back of my mind, like a low and steady hum, Elsie Kühn-Leitz sits in the Frankfurt jail. Toward the end of our weekday walks, when the baby drifts off, this is where my thoughts go. This creates strange overlays: Elsie and the beige awning of Pho Goodness, the Vietnamese soup place. Elsie and the Celebration of Light, the illuminated Christmas stars affixed to the brick façade of St. Paul's. Elsie and the homeless men who sit on the cement barriers in front of the hospital, derisive and self-derisive, watching the expensive coats hurrying to and from the coffee shops of Burrard.

One morning, the stroller nearly collides with a couple hurrying from the direction of the hospital. The man speaks rapidly and insistently, a rolling jerkiness to his stride that causes his sparse dark beard to approach and retreat from the woman's ear. The woman walks dead ahead, a white baby blanket clutched to her chest. It is impossible not to watch the woman, whose face, still full with the baby weight, is ravaged by a despair so deep and consuming, by a lifelessness that overtakes what might once have been a lively face, the grey eyes and dark hair, a white scar etched along her right jaw bone, the clutch of the blanket printed with small blue elephants. The pedestrians on Burrard give the couple a wide berth, sheltering from the draft of the city's Downtown Eastside, and I remember when we lived nearby and residential school stories of children taken and not returned could be heard in the screaming that splintered the night.

As the woman passes, I realize there is no baby in the blanket.

I begin to have a recurring nightmare I am on the SkyTrain, standing in the middle of the carriage, holding a metal pole with one hand, the stroller handle with the other. The baby sleeps in the stroller, wrapped in a white blanket, while I decipher the brightly coloured threads of the route map. In this dream, I follow the yellow line east, always east. When I look down, there is no baby in the blanket.

We see a good deal of my parents, who have the enviable advantage of practice. My father has an uncanny ability to rouse Tatianna from her naps without tears, speaking softly like some kind of baby whisperer summoned from a remote province. My mother expertly bounces the baby during the witching hour to rhythmic rock, turning up the volume to the latest Adele. "I'm not sure this will work," I say, the first time she pulls the video up on YouTube. But of course it does.

Singing, in general, soothes, and so I do it all the time, summoning up songs from my own childhood. But you can also, I learn, turn just about anything into a song, transform any object into something else. "We're going for a ride in a chariot, a chariot, a chariot," I sing to Tatianna as I push the stroller along Denman. "We're going for a ride in a chariot, all around the town." Head bobbing, eyes wide, she looks surprisingly convinced.

Throughout the winter, John and his business partner fulfill set-decor projects for the wave of historical epics that come streaming up the coast from Hollywood. On big, noisy machines, they make Egyptian pyramids and hieroglyphic walls, twenty-foot Corinthian columns and gothic gargoyles, carving the past out of great white blocks of styrofoam. At the quiet of my desk, I continue to reconstruct the events of 1943.

The Klapperfeld Police Prison where Elsie Kühn-Leitz was held was built in 1886. In the 1940s, the four-storey prison building and courtyard were vertically divided to create a section for men and a section for women. The fourth and top floor housed the Jewish section, where prisoners were incarcerated in tiny cages. Other parts of the jail, where political prisoners were held, contained a combination of private and communal cells, all rodent and bug-infested, most without running water. Gestapo interrogations and beatings were common.

In her essay, Elsie Kühn-Leitz reports her two regular interrogators were Inspector Gabusch and Inspector Thorn. The first is described as "an elegant man, a sadist who took pleasure in tormenting people."

Klapperfeld jail

(SOURCE: ERNST LEITZ FOUNDATION)

Inspector Thorn is "less polished, a true follower of Hitler's worldview." There is an impression the interrogations began slowly. Elsie Kühn-Leitz was a Leitz. Inspector Gabusch and Inspector Thorn ask their questions matter-of-factly, record her uncommunicative responses. Undeterred, they tell her of her father's stroke. But the jail also reveals an equivalency — how a system driven by categories of human and subhuman is also an interrogation room where no one is safe.

October 1943
Frankfurt, Germany

THE HALLWAY BETWEEN THE WOMEN'S PRISON and the Gestapo interrogation rooms is windowed. Elsie tries to slow her progress through this part of the corridor not, as Miss Hoog believes, because she is trying to delay the inevitable. Rather, it is because she can see the trees and, on the street beyond, regular people moving about, unburdened by the uncertainty of their fate. It offers Elsie some reassurance that the other world still exists. Even now, as she nears the end of the hallway, she can see a woman her own age in a black coat pause on the street to check for something in her handbag. It is such a mundane gesture, to walk on a street. To look inside one's own purse. But it is so distant, so exotic, that Elsie finds she cannot look away. She watches the woman in this strange act of normalcy until the windows are replaced by the grey paint that marks the beginning of the interrogation corridor.

Behind her, Miss Hoog directs Elsie to the right with some pressure on the metal where the handcuffs meet. Miss Hoog, with her chestnut hair and soft voice, is the least brutal of the kalfaktoren. She does not prod Elsie in the back with her stick. Unlike Miss Heldig, she does not seem to relish taking prisoners to the kitchens, serving them up to the interrogators. When they reach the interrogation room, Miss Hoog knocks, opens the door, pushes Elsie through the doorway and into the metal chair, firmly but without malice. She removes the handcuffs, nods at the two inspectors, and closes the door quietly behind her.

Elsie observes the inspectors, making an effort to quell the quaking of her limbs, to keep her breathing regular. Inspector Thorn is the shorter of the two, bustling and brutal, with a sandy tobacco-stained moustache, heavy around the middle, doctrinaire. A zealot with a short temper, Elsie has learned to navigate his questions carefully and dodge the worst of his brutality with a show of deference.

Inspector Gabusch is different. Tall, elegant, with sardonic intelligence, someone who has used the Nazi moment to give expression to his own pleasure in violence, loyal only to himself. She has come to realize that Gabusch enjoys these sessions, that for all his theatricality and menace he considers her a worthy adversary.

Elsie makes an effort to distance herself, to let go and find another place in time. She drifts for a moment, through the children's birthdays, the daily rhythm of the accounting office at Leitz Werke, and finds herself in Munich when she was a student. While Munich was never Berlin, there were still colourful corners in those days, and she and Berthe had often spent Saturdays strolling the city, walking through the patchwork of bakeries, coffee houses, and the brightly painted awnings of the clubs and cabarets.

Hitler was giving speeches regularly by then, though Elsie only saw him once, at the trial for his role staging the beer hall putsch, a poorly planned insurrection against the Weimar Republic in 1923. Hitler had led a mob of two thousand and been mildly injured. People had laughed. Here was a man who didn't even have the wherewithal to take over an army barrack. A beer hall! It was the trial itself that had made him a celebrity. Elsie and Berthe had pushed their way into the courtroom with some classmates from their introductory jurisprudence class, pressed in with other onlookers and the international press. On the stand, a tuft of hair had broken free and flopped around on Hitler's forehead like a dark fish. The state, Hitler had pronounced, arm waving like a deranged conductor, was there to provide the people with a food supply but not just food, also the position of power in the world, which was its due. These two things. Food and power. Power and food. Elsie had watched the onlookers, the accumulated losses of the war and the depression plain on their faces, hungry for both.

Afterward, in the pub: "To the beer hall!" someone had yelled, her classmates laughing over drinks, calling Hitler vulgar — "That ridiculous hair!" — making bets on just how quickly he would fade from the scene.

But the strange leniency of the judge and prosecutor, the oddly messianic tone of Hitler's speech, had made Elsie uneasy. "You may declare us guilty a thousand times, but the Goddess who presides over the Eternal Court of History . . . declares us guiltless."

Hitler had been convicted of treason but served only nine months of a five-year sentence. He was released on December 20, 1924, two days before Elsie's twenty-first birthday. On his release, he was photographed stiff-armed and magisterial, about to step into a Mercedes. The press gamely reproduced the photograph as it signalled Hitler's "release from the fortress." Only a very few noticed the photograph had been staged. The building in the background was not the Landsberg Fortress, where Hitler had comfortably dictated *Mein Kampf*, fruit and flowers in his cell, but rather the medieval Bavarian Gate at the southern entrance of the old town of Landsberg. At one of her father's Christmas dinner parties, one of the Leica photographers speculated that Heinrich Hoffmann had determined the old gate would make a far stronger visual statement about Hitler's reemergence and ambitions.

It wasn't long after this that the Nazis began murmuring about a third realm, the natural successor to the Holy Roman Empire and the more recent German Empire. The Third Reich would be a return to greatness, a glorious revival of German strength, the reemergence of global domination that would last one thousand years. And then the Nazis stopped murmuring and began to shout.

It is in this same voice that Thorn seems to be addressing Elsie now. While the other women describe the most unbearable physical torture, many of Elsie's own sessions have taken the form of the lecture, a peculiar blend of warped political science and perverted moral philosophy. When Thorn pulls something from the inside pocket of his coat, it is not, as Elsie has been half expecting, the slim metal instrument the other women have described, but rather a typed copy of some kind of document.

"Repeatedly, Frau Kühn-Leitz, you have told us that Hitler's law is against God's law. But the Bishop of Münster himself has spoken in favour of the Fatherland's campaign."

With an air of triumph, Thorn begins to read to her from the bishop's sermon, stressing the religious license of the war on the East.

"Does the bishop not convey the word of the God on Earth, Frau Kühn-Leitz?"

Elsie nods stiffly.

"And here he is speaking in favour of our campaign?"

Elsie nods.

"Is it not true that the bishop also rejects the socialism and decadence of the Weimar Republic?"

"Yes."

"And that, moreover, like our Leader, the bishop understands that the German side was defeated in 1918 not by outside forces but by enemies within the Fatherland itself: Jews, Bolsheviks, and deviants?"

The recitation of this popular lie is almost more than Elsie can cope with, but as the bishop has indeed espoused this theory of German defeat, she stays silent.

"That the bishop, like the Leader, saw the fundamental injustice of the Treaty of Versailles, the inhuman toll of the reparations exerted on the German people?

"Yes."

"So, how is it you claim Hitler's position is irreconcilable with religion? As a woman of God, you should be championing the Leader, using your influence to support the cause. Yet instead you spend your time abetting Jews who have sought to undermine the state. You provide aid to enemy Slavs on whom the bishop has proclaimed a just war."

At this point Thorn comes very close and Elsie can smell sweat and cigarettes.

"Has the bishop not spoken on these matters, Frau Kühn-Leitz?"

"Yes," Elsie says. "Yes, he has."

Thorn smirks, sensing victory. Gabusch watches Elsie carefully from behind the desk.

Elsie knows she should hold her silence. That arguments with someone like Thorn are as pointless as a fight with a rabid dog. That resistance, moreover, will cause the dog to turn its madness and fury on her.

"But the bishop has also spoken out against the Nazi campaign to euthanize the disabled. And forced sterilizations. And most definitely the bishop has spoken out against disappearances without trial. There is no basis for dominion without justice."

Thorn looks at Elsie in disgust, as though she were a wilful and disappointing student.

"Do you know what Verschärfte Vernehmung means, Frau Kühn-Leitz? It is the power of enhanced interrogation given to us by Müller himself. Your actions have made you part of the resistance, which means we have every justification we need. You have been treated well here, out of respect for your father. But there are barracks at Dachau reserved specifically for religious deviants, Frau Kühn-Leitz. How difficult do you think it would be to add your name to the transport list?"

Elsie looks at Thorn. Yesterday it had been Eliza, a Christian woman married to a Jewish man. Her weeping as she was led down the prison corridor by Miss Hoog had chilled Elsie so profoundly that she had had to sit on the bed to keep her legs from collapsing. Her reaction, she knew, was only part sympathy. Having faced the possibility of her own deportation alone in her cell allows her to hold her silence now.

Thorn has played his trump card. When it fails to work, Elsie has only a moment before his arm rises across his body and then comes down heavily across her face, the force of the blow cracking her skull roughly to the side.

"You zealots are all the same, tainted by your commitment to Christ, controlled by foreign forces. Where is your loyalty to Germany and the German people? To the Fatherland?"

A second blow lands above Elsie's cheekbone, and she feels the skin tear against Thorn's ring as a high-pitched whine fills her ears. There is a sharp knock on the door, and a Gestapo captain's head appears. The captain glances at Gabusch, who makes a minute shrug.

"There is a telephone call coming through for the prisoner," the captain says.

Then, looking dispassionately at Elsie he says, "Come with me, Thorn."

Refusing to look at Elsie, Thorn marches smartly out of the room. The door closes behind him.

Behind the desk, Gabusch sighs, adjusts his weight in his chair. "I am afraid my colleagues have their boorish side, Frau Kühn-Leitz. A lack of subtlety, as they say."

Elsie looks blankly at Gabusch, who rises from behind the desk, removes a handkerchief from his breast pocket, and presses it gently to the cut above her right cheekbone. Elsie can feel the warmth of Gabusch's hand through the cloth. The moment, almost human, is splintered by the ring of the telephone on the desk. Gabusch backs away, folds the handkerchief with her blood on it, places it back into the pocket of his uniform. With his other hand, he picks up the receiver. After listening for a moment, he hands the receiver to Elsie, the black cord stretched taut across the distance between the desk and her chair. The telephone is not yet to her ear when she hears her father's voice.

"Elsie? Are you there?"

"Father."

"Are you all right?"

Elsie can hear the slight stammer in his speech, an effect of his stroke, a confirmation that Gabusch has told the truth.

"Yes, Father," she says as steadily as she can.

"Elsie. Listen, Direktor Hof has agreed to help us. He is working to secure your release. The way we do — you understand?"

Elsie understands. Hof and her father are working on an enormous bribe.

"Yes, I understand."

"Elsie. I need you —"

Her father's voice is replaced by a click. Elsie stares at the receiver, unable to believe she has been speaking with her father, unable to bear he is gone. Her thoughts travel to Haus Friedwart, the damage of the stroke, the softness of her children's hair under the brush.

When her attention returns to the room, Elsie realizes Gabusch is watching her. He approaches her softly, concern painted in his eyes, which for the first time Elsie realizes are blue at the centre and hazel around the edges. He travels around the desk, takes the receiver from her hand, replaces it in the cradle. He moves behind her, hands on her shoulders, his fingers on her neck soft from regular care. Elsie can feel the thinness of her own bones, the narrow circumference of her neck stiffening now, from the impact of Thorn's blows. The room begins to rock, ever so slightly, beneath her feet.

"Your father no doubt tried to reassure you, Frau Kühn-Leitz, but let me be clear that you cannot be released without my say-so."

The small hairs at the base of her skull begin to rise as Gabusch strokes the tendons rigid above her collarbone.

"The children must miss you. Your son — Knut, is it? And those lovely girls. Such fond memories, I have, of my own school days. Of course I was just a youth then, nervous of girls and their propriety."

Gabusch's manicured fingernails trace the top of her sternum, then travel farther as he rubs the flat of his hand down the bony plateau of her chest. Elsie feels her breath falter as Gabusch transmits the full intention of the threat, as if she hadn't heard what happens in these rooms, as if she didn't know. After a long moment, Gabusch pulls his hand from her shift as though from a bucket of water and returns to the edge of the desk.

"It is very simple, Frau Kühn-Leitz. In all these cases, it comes down to names."

That night, as she lies on her cot, Elsie turns the interrogation over in her mind. As the bombers begin their descent on Frankfurt, the first crash of an exploding building, as her cell begins to shake, the women to scream, plaster and dust to fall from the ceiling, it comes to Elsie in a flash that this is hell and Gabusch is the devil himself. Elsie begins the Lord's Prayer, which swiftly turns into improvised pleading with God as a nearby building is hit and the reverberation makes the floor lurch. Suddenly, there is a light and Miss Hoog appears with a clatch of keys.

"Move, Leitz. Now," she yells, grabbing Elsie by the wrist. Together, the two women run down the corridor and Miss Hoog stumbles against one of the communal cell doors, causing the cover of the peephole to sway. Elsie sees a familiar eye pressed against the opening, filled with rage and resentment. Miss Hoog hurries Elsie down a flight of stairs, opens a door. Together they squeeze in among the bodies already occupying the air raid shelter. Miss Hoog closes the door, and in the dim light, Elsie realizes she is among the female guards. Miss Hoog passes her a black medical bag from where it had been hanging on a nail on the wall. "New orders," she says. "From now on, you are our first aid attendant."

In the semi-darkness, Elsie feels two things at once: the great relief of being out of danger and the steady certainty of the grief this salvation will cause her. As the bombs fall, it is the twisted, angry eye of the railway guard that floods Elsie's mind, her face pressed hard against the door between them.

June 2012
Vancouver, Canada

THE STREETLIGHT SHINES INTO THE BEDROOM, thin bars of light between the slats of the blinds, somewhere between night and morning. Wallet. E-tickets. Giraffe. I list the things the baby and I will need for our flight to Toronto at noon. I can see John breathing deeply where the white sheet cuts a diagonal across his blue t-shirt. Envy him. *Just sleep*, I tell myself. *Find a point in time and drift.*

In those early days when we had time, John and I would take the tiny boat across False Creek. We would buy ingredients for elaborate meals in the covered market on Granville Island: fat floured bands of fresh linguine, basil overflowing from a barrel, parmesan in thick, chalky blocks, gravity-defying towers of bing cherries, local spot prawns in chips of ice. I remember John buying a handful of prawns with a green twenty, how disconcerted I was when his change was returned in silver coins, remembering another time: the crude spray paint of the plywood sign in the clearing above the ferry parking lot, the men with rough hands who would sell prawns, still wriggling, in white plastic bags off the tailgates of battered pick-ups. "$5/lb" the spray paint said — "What's a lib?" I asked my mother. The way she would haul the heavy bag into the kitchen, the sharp knife, the alien heads that would jump of their own accord from the chopping block into the sink. *The market is for tourists*, I said to myself, though what tourists do with raw shellfish on their kitchenless holidays, I could not say. Still, surrounded by such abundance, it seemed obtuse to dwell.

The things I learned about John's family over these meals were significant, though not in ways I fully understood. His parents were older than mine and he was the fourth child rather than the first and only. And so it was that his father, fresh out of Assiniboia, was readied for war as a sixteen-year-old at a camp in the Connaught Ranges, but was never deployed to Europe. He and John's mother were childhood neighbours in Saskatchewan and met again as students in Toronto. John's mother was a nurse. John's father worked for Chrysler, fielding customer complaints with jokes and bonhomie for thirty-three years. When I first met them at their home in White Rock over a casserole of chicken in Campbell's mushroom soup, Iceberg salad, and white dinner rolls, what I was struck by was their optimism, their sense of their own inevitable good fortune, the casual way they believed it would never run out. I had never spent time with people of that generation who felt this way. And I saw the way that John, a serendipitous surprise after three older siblings, had been nursed on this faith, this resilient milk in endless supply, and grown strong and sure on it.

June 2012
Niagara Falls, Canada

MY GRANDMOTHER SITS IN A FOLDING lawn chair, which I fished out of
her basement earlier in the day. I sit on a blanket on the lawn, the baby
sleeping in my arms. We are in the public rose garden, across the street
from the Falls.

In many ways, our visit is the same as last year's, but there are
changes. There is the baby, of course, the uncomplicated way her
fingers reach out to grasp my grandmother's grey curls. The other differences are more subtle: my grandmother's long silences, the traces of
potting soil on the carpet, the half-filled bag of nectarines and quart of
milk in an otherwise empty fridge. But most of all there is the distance
in my grandmother, the undeniable truth that my mother, Tatianna,
and I have travelled four thousand kilometres and cannot reach her
still. After three days, I cease to think of the past as a shared thing
between us. It is a war and one I am not winning.

I take her abandonment personally, though this is absurd and
I know it. I am irritated and far less gentle than I should be on this

outing, which is supposed to be a fun excursion to the Falls to "get out of the house," my mother says, with a levity that poorly conceals her anguish. At the moment, she is parking the Oldsmobile at the new casino. The casino has replaced a giant amusement park as the Falls' central attraction. Even now I look over to catch sight of the giant Ferris wheel, listen for the screams of roller coaster riders. But it's gone now, and the depression of this, iced by my irritation, gives all my movements a sharpness that I know is unbecoming, to say the least.

Tatianna wakes from her nap and reaches for the gold chain around my neck. Beside me, my grandmother stares into the steady cascade of the waterfall. The smell of roses in the heat is overwhelming.

"Tatianna took a step on her own," I say.

"Good. That good."

"Everyone's coming for lunch next week — Laurie and Jerry, Alex and Debi, the cousins."

"Yes, will be nice."

"What would you like to serve?"

My grandmother shrugs. "Whatever you think, Sasha."

She continues to watch and not watch the water falling. Tatianna begins to fuss. I suddenly feel very young and not just a little bit afraid. I look down at Tatianna, distracted now by the bobbing tenacity of a dandelion stem she has grabbed in her fist.

"Baba — Frau Elsie. Did you ever see her again?"

This time my grandmother's gaze shifts from the falling water. For the first time this visit, I see all of her in her eyes. For the first time, she looks straight at me.

June, 1945
Wetzlar, Germany

IN THE END, IRINA AND SERGEI use the British soldiers' money to buy
train tickets from Turnhout to Wetzlar. With no plans, no belongings,
and only a few coins left, they have nowhere else to go but back. The
train ride is an agony of wondering if they will be caught by a Russian
patrol, but though the train is packed with the displaced, no one checks
for papers. At the Wetzlar station, Irina and Sergei climb the road up
the hill. When they make the last turn into the driveway that opens out
onto the expansive lawn of Haus Friedwart, Irina sees Heidi and the
children playing in the garden. The children run over and Heidi hugs
Irina, shakes hands with Sergei.

"I can't believe you're here," Heidi says. "We heard you were taken
by the Russians!"

Irina distracts Heidi with talk about the house, to keep her from
saying anything else in front of the children. Karin and Cornelia
take Irina's hands. Knut shows Sergei his toy airplane as they walk
up the stairs to the front door. Sergei tries to keep his eye on the

plane, but mostly he is staring at the house, overwhelmed by its size and grandeur.

Friedrich opens the door, Frau Vogel behind him. "Irina . . ." he says. Irina is surprised by the relief in Friedrich's face, which floods his features then quickly retreats when he greets Sergei. Flustered, Irina turns to Frau Vogel. In response to a question Irina has yet to ask, Frau Vogel bows her head toward Irina's so that she can speak softly in her ear.

"We don't know what happened to Marina and Leah. They went down to the camp to get information about their villages, and they didn't come back. I can't imagine they would have left without saying goodbye, but if the Russians took them or there was some opportunity to escape . . ."

Suddenly Frau Elsie is there, her hand on Irina's shoulder. Irina is conscious of how unkept she must look, still in the auxiliary uniform. Frau Elsie herself is wearing a soft grey suit with a clean white blouse. Her hair has grown into a bob that curls around her ears. She directs Irina and Sergei to the downstairs quarters to get cleaned up. Frau Vogel fetches them some clothes, a white blouse, tweed skirt and jacket for Irina, a brown suit for Sergei, a matching pair of shoes from Herr Leitz's closet. When they have bathed and changed, they sit with Frau Elsie at the kitchen table beside the familiar green sideboard.

"You could stay," Frau Elsie says.

Irina pauses. This has been her hope, of course, that they could hide inside Haus Friedwart until it is safe to move on. But now that they are here, sitting at the kitchen table, the way Frau Elsie looks calm and settled, beyond the worst of what the jail has done to her, the way Sergei is a stranger here — it takes her a moment, but Irina shakes her head.

Frau Elsie pauses, then pulls a stack of bills from her pocketbook.

"You have no idea what's coming," she says. "Money helps."

Sergei stares at the money for a moment, then takes it from Frau Elsie's hand with a bow of his head, folds the bills, and puts them in the pocket of Herr Leitz's brown suit. Irina and Sergei both murmur their thanks as the three of them rise from the table. Irina looks around the kitchen, at the green stove and Frau Lichen's cutting knife sitting on the counter. When Frau Elsie hugs her, Irina is plunged into the scent of lilies. It is the most difficult of the goodbyes before she leaves with Sergei.

July, 2012
Vancouver, Canada

"HOW IS SHE?" I ASK.

After only two weeks home from our trip, my mother has flown back to Niagara Falls and is standing outside my grandmother's hospital room. I tuck the phone between my ear and shoulder and gesture to John to take over watching Tatianna, who is piling soft blocks in a corner of the living room. I move into the bedroom and close the door.

"Stable," my mother says. "Sleeping. She was alone in the house and fell down those stairs between the bedrooms and the living room. She thought she heard something in the night."

"We shouldn't have —"

"The doctor says the x-rays show a newly broken vertebra, along with two other breaks, earlier in her life. Those early breaks were never diagnosed. She always just kept going."

"How is she otherwise?"

"In and out. Confused. They're giving her morphine, plus the doctor says there's a dislocation factor, being out of her house. She's been talking about Germany, when the war ended."

"But she doesn't talk about that."

"No —"

"How are you?" I ask.

"Okay. It's hard. They've got her on the first floor of the hospital, and it's cold down here. She's been sleeping with the sheet over her head. When I first got here I thought —"

"Oh God."

"I know. Wait a minute. She's awake."

I hear a shuffling as my mother moves into the hospital room.

"Mom, are you awake?"

"Yes. Yes. I okay. Baby . . ."

My mother speaks into the receiver again.

"She's asking for the baby."

"Tatianna?"

"I don't think so. Let me call you back."

March 30, 1946
Polish Displaced Persons Camp,
Wetzlar, Germany

WHEN IRINA WAKES, SHE IS SWEATING. She understands that she is in
hospital by the rows of beds and the antiseptic smell. She remembers
the visit to Haus Friedwart, the scent of lilies. And she remembers,
now, the decision to return to the Polish camp, to try again. For
months, she and Sergei have worked on their Polish, paid for advanced
information from camp officials, hidden in the woods whenever the
Russians roll in with their trucks.

"Where is my baby?" Irina asks a passing nurse, trying to surface
above the panic.

The nurse's eyes crinkle, whether with amusement or annoyance
Irina cannot tell.

"He's in the nursery. I'll get him for you."

Irina feels ill and feverish, and the previous day comes back in
flashes: the seizing abdominal pain the hospital staff dismissed as
hunger pains. "What baby? You're thin as a rake."

The nurse returns with Alexandre. He is sleeping, and his regular little breaths are audible. The nurse places him in Irina's arms. Most of the patients are sleeping, soft mounds under white sheets. Beyond the quiet of the hospital, Irina hears men laughing. She looks up at the nurse.

"Your husband bought a barrel of wine. Half the camp is drunk on it. They've been at it all night."

The nurse's tone is severe. Irina tucks her chin and smiles down at the baby. A small group of men begin reciting in Russian, their voices careening into well-known phrases.

> *In alien lands I keep the body*
> *Of ancient native rites and things:*
> *I gladly free a little bird*
> *In celebration of the spring.*

When Irina wakes, Sergei is standing above her bed, smelling of wine, his hair dishevelled.

"I have to go," he says.

Irina is flooded with adrenaline. Sergei is going off somewhere with his friends when the baby has just arrived? But Sergei holds up his hand before she can speak.

"There was a Polish commandant at the party last night. He was very drunk. He told me the Russians are coming today. My name is on their list, Irina."

Irina feels her whole body seize. Sergei is still talking, so rapidly she can hardly take it in.

"The doctor says you can't travel, but only men are listed this time. I have arranged for the doctor to keep you here, to treat you under a Polish name. I'm going to hide in another camp with Pyoter Korban. His wife is staying here and she has agreed to check on you. I promise you'll be fine. I'll be back when I can."

Again Irina begins to say something, but Sergei is already leaving, kissing her cheek, hurrying out the clinic doors. Irina drops her head back onto her pillow. She has a high fever and heavy bleeding but cannot sleep for worry.

"You need to rest," the doctor tells her. He is in his mid-forties with dark hair and brown eyes, one of which wanders benignly. "This emotional upset isn't good for you or the baby. I told Sergei I would look after you." This doctor is from Georgia, Gregor Vladyavich, a friend.

In the afternoons, Pyoter Korban's wife, Katya, comes to sit with Irina. Pyoter and Katya have the room next to them in the camp. Pyoter and Sergei would sometimes sit out in the hallway, talking, but Katya has kept to herself. She is thirty-five, twelve years older than Irina, but already her face is heavily lined and her blue eyes have a strange, watery quality. There is so much sadness around her that at first Irina is worried it will affect the baby, like a draft. But Katya is good with Alexandre, squeezing his little feet, speaking to him gently, rocking him through his colic, and Irina becomes grateful for her visits. As Irina grows stronger, they talk for longer periods. At first, Katya is hesitant, saying little. But one day something penetrates the story at the very heart of her, and she tells it to Irina with her eyes fixed on the wall.

"Our family was better off than most in Ukraine. We weren't really wealthy, but we had a nice house, someone to cook for us. I used to be glad for our good fortune, two boys and a daughter, another on the way. Pyoter's father had connections, and it looked like the future was secure."

Katya holds the corner of Irina's bedsheet in her hands. She folds and unfolds the corner several times.

"The Communists came for us in 1929 and sent all of us to a labour camp in Siberia. They said we were class traitors. We tried. We gave the children our rations, but it was so cold, they couldn't grow. They all died there, one after the other. First little Anya, eyes wide open, then the two boys within a month of each other. Their bodies froze before we could bury them. The baby was stillborn. Pyoter's parents died. People were dropping like flies, from the cold and hunger, the work."

Katya looks up. Her eyes are dry, her voice detached as though describing an episode from someone else's life.

"Pyoter and I knew we had to escape, and one day, in the middle of the night, we made a run for it. We crept out of the camp when one of the guards was sleeping and we took the train to the next village. Pyoter and I parted and made plans to meet again in the next city. We knew they were after us. We lived like that for eight years, always running, always waiting for them to come for us."

Irina looks at Katya, wondering if this life on the run will be her life with Sergei.

"And then, just when we were starting to think that the secret police had stopped looking for us, we were rounded up in a nighttime raid by the Germans."

Katya gives a short laugh.

"And so we ended up in Germany, kept by German soldiers, until the war was over. It was a break, really, from worrying about the Russians. But now the war is over and here we are — pretending to be Polish, just waiting for the Russians to come for us again."

The two women sit together, Irina propped up in her hospital bed, Katya in the chair beside her. For a long time, neither of them speaks.

July 2012
Vancouver, Canada

MY MOTHER SPENDS SEVERAL WEEKS IN Niagara Falls. During the day, she sits beside my grandmother's hospital bed. In the evenings, she tends my grandmother's garden. At night, she sleeps in my grandmother's empty house. During visits, my grandmother slips in and out. When she wakes, she is glad, grateful my mother has been able to find her in the hospital of the Polish camp.

My mother relays this information over my grandmother's cordless phone, sitting in the backyard in the sultry evening air, looking out over the neighbour's tomato plants. These conversations make me realize what I have missed. After we talk, I push aside some notes on Frau Elsie's work assignment in the sewing room at the Klapperfeld jail and pick up the small stack of photographs of my grandparents' first few months in Canada. I look at the pictures taken at the Falls.

The photographs with Pyoter and Katya Korban in them make a new kind of sense — the rigid, bitter lines in his face, the perpetual sadness in hers. But the images of my grandparents look different, too.

Even as they stand dazed in the morning sun, their hands are anything but still. They clutch their children in their arms or grasp their small fingers in front of the guard railing. They look ahead, into the lens of the camera, tense with expectation. Except when these photographs are taken in profile. When my grandmother looks sideways at the camera, it captures something deeply wary and unspeakably haunted. It is only in stringing these photographs together across the surface of my desk that I begin to see what combination of emotion, what desire and struggling fear dominated those early years, what shadows played across her hopes for this new place, what echoes, God knows, she heard in the steady click of the shutter.

October 1943
Frankfurt, Germany

ELSIE HEARS THE LOCK CATCH AS Miss Hoog closes the door behind her. She looks around, taking stock of the sewing room. The room is rectangular, with sewing machines lining the long walls and a wooden worktable at the far end. More than anything else, Elsie is struck by the light and realizes that above the worktable are three narrow glass panes, the only windows in the jail other than in the hallway leading to the interrogation rooms. There are a dozen prisoners working, some of them dressed in nothing but rags. The baroness and Isabella are at the long table at the far end and Elsie moves to join them. Wedged behind the second-to-last sewing machine on the right, Kathe kicks out at Elsie's leg as she passes, but Elsie dodges her foot with a step to the side. Even as Elsie makes her way over to the baroness and Isabella, she can feel the railway guard's eyes and becomes acutely aware that Miss Hoog is well down the corridor by now.

"Transferred at last," the baroness says warmly, making room for Elsie to sit on the bench beside her. Across the table Isabella, lean and straight-backed, smiles at her.

"What are you working on?" Elsie asks her, genuinely curious about the wooden sticks and balls of material scattered on the top of the worktable.

"We make toys at this end," Isabella says, holding up her creation in a way that makes Elsie realizes the ball is a doll's head. The sewing machines are for mending uniforms."

"It's preferable to make toys," the baroness says. "At least they are for the officers' children, who have no stake in all of this. When we mend uniforms, I leave pins in the sleeves."

Isabella looks around and shushes the older woman. "Baroness, please."

A sly look comes into Thusnelda's face. "My heart will get me before the Nazis. That's the one revenge of ill health. Save your concern for Elsie. When you walked in, Kathe looked like she wanted to sew your face to the table."

Glancing in Kathe's direction, Isabella asks, "How is she still here and not at Ravensbrück? That's where they usually send women communists."

"How do you think?" the baroness responds. "It's the same here as everywhere. Everyone is trading information to gain some advantage." She turns back to Elsie. "Now that you're here, watch how Isabella makes her dolls. They are the most charming thing to come out of this place."

Elsie looks over to see that Isabella has transformed the stick and ball with a bit of lace, wrapping the raw materials of the head to create a bonnet.

"I always do the face last," Isabella says, picking up a needle and some black embroidery thread. She gradually transforms the doll into something with an almost living expression.

"It's beautiful, Isabella," Elsie says, meaning it.

"Thank you. It's important to me that each one is unique."

A sudden sadness comes over the young woman, something hopeless that seeps across the table. Of all the women, it is Isabella who is sent most often to Jager with his iron chains and bathtub of freezing water. The baroness, with an eye on Isabella, fastens a belt around the waist of the doll she is making and begins singing in a soft, low voice.

> *Once there was a blonde boy.*
> *He begged so sweetly.*
> *Mamatschi, give me a little horse.*
> *A little horse would be my paradise.*

Around the room, women join in singing the well-known folk song about a boy and his mother, though they keep sewing, their eyes on their work.

> *So then the father got a pair of white horses made of marzipan.*
> *The boy looks at them, and cries.*
> *He says, "I didn't want this kind of horses."*
> *Mamatschi, give me a little horse.*
> *A little horse would be my paradise.*
> *Mamatschi, "I didn't want this kind of horses."*

January 2012
Vancouver, Canada

AFTER EIGHT MONTHS OF HOSPITALIZATION, it becomes clear my grandmother will not return to her house. My uncle and aunt take on the daunting task of emptying it. Some clothes, framed photographs, and hand-crocheted blankets are set aside for when my grandmother is settled somewhere new. A few things, including my grandmother's lace tablecloth, are put into a box for my mother. Some things go to my aunt and uncle's home and some to my cousins'. But overwhelmingly, the physical remnants of my grandparents' lives cannot be accommodated in the houses of others. A great deal is given to the Salvation Army. But the rest goes into two 14' x 12' mobile dumpsters that my uncle has hauled away.

There are a number of things I never see again: the assorted perfume bottles on the gold-rimmed tray, the jars of pickled beets and marinated peppers, my grandfather's plaid work shirts, the peach bedspread, the amber glass fruit bowl and its plastic fruit, the matryoshka doll, my grandmother's white gardening hat, the cuckoo clock, the drawer full of grocery coupons, the half-used bottle of Oil of Olay.

I never again see the photograph where my grandmother and I look so much alike, the one taken in Fontaine l'Évêque in 1947. I have only the remembered look on my uncle's face to confirm the resemblance was everything I thought it was.

When my mother flies east again, it is to see my grandmother and help with the sale of the house. The day before the first open house, she calls me on Skype. She walks through the empty rooms with her laptop. It is the first time I have seen the house since it has been emptied.

"Slow down. Everything is blurry."

My mother slows, the image becomes more integrated, and I focus in on a plain beige room with bare walls.

"Is that the living room?"

"Yes," my mother says, rotating the computer. The mirror over the couch is gone. So are all the family photos, my parents' wedding picture, the painting of my mother and uncle as teenagers.

"Wow," I say. "It looks completely different."

"I know. I can't say I care for it. It looks sterile, really. But the real estate agent says that's what sells. People want to be able to project their own lives onto blank surfaces rather than compete with the life of the seller."

"If I were a buyer, I think I would prefer the character of Baba's things."

"I told the real estate agent the same thing. She said I was unique."

We laugh a little and my mother wanders into the kitchen. All my grandmother's spices are gone from the shelf behind the stove. A cranberry candle has been placed in their stead. Three bottles of Evian water are grouped between the burners.

"Have you told Baba?"

My mother pauses. "Not yet," she says. "Not until she has a place to go. The doctors say there's no possibility she can come home, and she knows that, but we haven't brought up the house. Alex is working on getting a room in a nursing home close to Debi's parents so that they can visit everyone at once."

It takes me a moment to take this in, the house that is no longer my grandmother's, the permanent move into care.

My mother turns the laptop around so that it is now her face I see on the screen. She looks chilled in the watery light coming through the kitchen window.

"Take a sweater to the hospital," I say.

She smiles slightly and nods. We say goodbye. Her face disappears from the screen.

October 1943
Frankfurt, Germany

EVERY SECOND SATURDAY, A HANDFUL OF prisoners are allowed to bathe in the basement, two or three women to a tub. The water is cold and the tubs are cramped, but it does provide some relief from the bug bites and the smells. Elsie tries to use the shock of the water to rid herself of the residue of the interrogation the day before. There is never enough soap, and Elsie longs for something to scrub away the desolation.

Cramped in beside her, Elsie observes the signs of undernourishment in the limp breasts and protruding rib cages of Isabella and the Baroness Thusnelda. Though modesty is a long-discarded luxury, most of the women keep their focus inward. As she washes her back, Elsie feels the bruise at the base of her spine from the railway guard's punch in the sewing room the day before. It had been a blind assault, coming as Elsie reached for a piece of muslin, and had produced a painful vibration from the base of her skull to her toes, over which Kathe had said distinctly in her ear, "Capitalist bitch," before pushing her way past. *So much for a community of women,* Elsie thinks grimly.

As her fingertips reach the tender middle of the bruise, the discomfort causes her to look up.

Arms wrapped around her knees, neck at an unnatural angle, Isabella stares into the bath water. Her eyes are wide open and staring, her lips stretched into a grimace, distorting the lines of her face. Suddenly, her chest begins to heave in spasmodic bursts and at first Elsie thinks she is crying. It is not uncommon for women to break down in the baths, away from the eyes of the guards. It takes Elsie a moment to realize the young woman is laughing, gripped by some kind of manic hysteria.

Elsie touches the baroness's leg and together they pull Isabella from the water and slide down onto the tile floor outside the tub. The sound of metal scraping across the floor above pushes Isabella further into her mania, and she begins to writhe, the back of her head rhythmically banging against the outside edge of the tub. Without hesitation, the baroness smacks Isabella across the face. The young woman looks stunned, shrinks back against the white industrial surface. The laughter stops.

Taking one of Isabella's arms and gesturing to Elsie to take the other, the baroness pulls Isabella to her feet and the three of them make their way to the far wall where their clothes are hanging on pegs. The baroness and Elsie pull their shifts over their own damp bodies and quickly clothe Isabella, the baroness speaking in a low, insistent voice masked by the sound of running water.

"Don't do that. You think it's bad for you now? If they decide you've turned into an idiot, you'll be on the next train to the camps."

Isabella continues to look numbly ahead, and Thusnelda softens her tone.

"I know," she says as Isabella's face begins to fold into new lines, hard now and full of rage and despair. "But you must pull yourself together, even here. Not everyone is losing weight as we are, which means some are trading favours or information for food. So I need you to put on your shoes now, before anyone sees you."

Awkward and angry, Isabella reaches for the black shoes beneath her peg. The baroness catches Elsie's eye with a warning look.

It is not until exercise the next day that the two are able to talk. The sky is leaden and heavy, another wall in addition to the four that surround the yard.

"It's Jager," the baroness says to Elsie. "He's breaking her."

"Why? She's not a spy. Anyone can see that."

"There's no deterrent. To them she is subhuman. She has no family or connections. Where there are no protections, there are no limits to evil."

In the other life, Elsie would have found this statement melodramatic. She would have argued some innate human goodness.

"Don't underestimate what it means to be a Leitz or a Thusnelda, even in here. Why do you think Kathe resents you? Even in the worst of circumstances it is unlikely we will see the worst of the worst. But Isabella . . . We must do what we can to hold her together. The bombing is intensifying. If she can hold on, she might make it."

Elsie looks across the yard to where Isabella, pale and withdrawn, walks unseeingly beside her exercise partner. The young woman walks with a strange shuffle, as though dropped into a lunar landscape.

February 2013
Vancouver, Canada

IN FEBRUARY, THE RAIN COMES THE way it only comes on the coast, in transparent sheets of celluloid. John pleads laundry but I decide to press on with a Saturday morning walk. By the time Tatianna and I reach the bottom of the hill at Denman and Comox, I know I have made a mistake. The promise has gone out of English Bay and the water is grey and flat, the palm trees limp with the weight of the rain. Across the street, curled bodies in sleeping bags fill the doorways like red and blue snowdrifts. The windows of the corner commercial space are covered in brown paper, another restaurant gone under, North Indian, though we only ate there once.

The waitress, I remember, had been from Alberta, a recent transplant with her young son, older than Tatianna by a few years. She watched Tatianna devour a spicy rogan josh, my daughter's two-year-old face bright with the heat of it. It was a dish the waitress's son wouldn't touch though the owners were kind and supplied leftovers at the end of every shift. And so it went: the job, the neighbourhood, her son's elementary school. People were nice. Friendly. Her son was happy enough, though the principal had put a recent end to field trips. It wasn't that some parents wouldn't pay the ten dollars for the trip to the museum. They always found the money. It was that the next week there was no protein in their children's lunches.

I push the stroller past the restaurant's darkened windows in the direction of the low-rise mall. In the artificial warmth of the entry-way, I unzip the rain shield. Tatianna smiles the smile of the newly rescued. We pass through the turnstile of the No Frills, and I navigate the stroller through aisles that are packed with people, the lines longer and less patient than they once were. I pick up canned tomatoes and a box of linguine. At the back of the store, I reach the shelf that holds the German rye and my eye flicks over the yellow price marker. The loaf, already more expensive than it is in Niagara Falls, is $1.20 more this week.

We wait in line at the checkout. I pack up the groceries and roll the stroller back out onto Denman. Though it is still morning, the streetlamps are on and both they and the streetlights are smeared by the rain. I long to stop in on someone but realize I have nowhere to go. Most of our friends have left the neighbourhood and moved east — to the east of the city or the east of the country — looking for that elusive place where a small house might still be considered a viable part of middle-class life.

I tell myself to stop, that it's just the weather. That a normal amount of perspective is in order. Summer will come and everyone will stream down to the beaches and everything will look different. As my grand-mother says, we are lucky. But these peripheral accumulations give way to white noise that borders on migraine. The noise is made of questions, half-formed and insistent, questions about the limits of the coast and failed utopias, about vanishing opportunities for the newly arrived and the newly disillusioned, for men with strong backs, once breadwinners and union workers, lost now in the haze of global trade, the gig economy, and opioid oblivion, even as a red tide has begun to claim this city, at intersections and convenience stores, something easy among us turning into something harder and disconnected, something uneasy among us growing softly more extreme.

We reach the apartment and I do my best to shake off the rain. The stroller is too wet to bring in, so I leave it in the hall, balance the baby and the bag of groceries, put the keys in the lock. Inside, the apartment smells like warm dryer sheets. John folds laundry in front of the TV, pairing Tatianna's small white socks with CNN. Onscreen, an American governor, full of messianic outrage, rides the runoff of the 2008 financial crisis.

I put the yellow bag on the kitchen floor, where the raindrops immediately start to pool on the laminate.

"Anything exciting?" John calls out.

"The rye has gone up by over a dollar." Even to my own ears this sounds abrupt and out of tune and I wonder why I am fixating on something so minor.

"We can afford it."

"That's not the point. It's more than 15 percent in one week."

John nods, acknowledging this, balls up a pair of his gym socks and tosses them on a pile. Tatianna squirms in my arms, a reminder she is still in her rain suit. The TV seems to be getting louder. I stare at John across the kitchen counter. He looks carefully at my face. There is an increase in attention, then a softening in his eyes, a landing point, that inherited certainty that everything will be fine.

"Hey," he says gently. "It's just bread."

November 1943
Frankfurt, Germany

WHEN ISABELLA DISAPPEARS, IT IS WITH none of the screaming that most often marks a transport to Auschwitz. One morning she is taken to interrogation, singing softly to herself, looking vaguely past the cells of the other inmates as though over a pastoral field. By exercise time, she has not returned.

"She won't come back," the baroness says as she and Elsie walk around the exercise track.

Elsie tells herself to be grateful for small things. That she has yet to be transferred to a concentration camp. For the small moments of solidarity in the sewing room, despite Kathe's fists and taunts. That somewhere in the world outside her father is working to secure her release. She recites these things as evidence of God's mercy. But as the cells of the women she has come to know — the laundress, the teacher — are emptied, replaced by the bodies of new women, these beliefs are swept away by the cold certainty there is no mercy. She no longer thinks of the prison as the most concentrated expression of the

Reich. It is merely a holding cell for what comes next. Lying on her cot, staring at the cracks in the ceiling, the boiler now speaks a different message. It tells her not to worry. That the children are old enough. That they are strong.

Everything becomes quieter. The sight of blood on a billy stick ceases to shock her. In interrogation, she stares vacantly at Gabusch, no longer responds to Thorn's hysterical questions. She sees Gabusch's disappointment, senses his waning interest. Occasionally a voice in her head will tell her to answer a question, to put up some kind of fight. But she is simply too tired. The Gestapo officers look silly in their black outfits, like mimes on an absurdist stage. As she leaves the interrogation room, she hears Thorn murmur to Gabusch that they should send her on to Jager. Gabusch looks at her thoughtfully for a moment. Elsie does not hear his response.

Elsie becomes aware she is the baroness's new project. "Don't drown in here, Elsie. You have to swim to survive," she exhorts during exercise. Elsie nods, glad that whatever is happening with her seems to have roused her friend to her former fighting self.

As Miss Heldig marches her through the windowed corridor between the prison and the interrogation rooms, Elsie considers throwing herself out the window, surrendering to the air and clouds of the November sky. Surely this would be better than the days of suspended, silent hysteria, the nights of bombs falling, the women around her disappearing into the night. Surely it would be better for her family to stop wondering about her, worrying about her, every day a strain on the children, on her father's health. Even if she were to be released someday, she knows she will never be the same.

Miss Heldig pushes Elsie brutally against the cement wall beside the interrogation room wall and her chin scuffs against its roughness. *It doesn't matter*, Elsie thinks. *The ground will be softer. The ground is ready for her, ready to take her. The earth alone has compassion.* Inside, Elsie knows that Thorn and Gabusch are waiting, planning whatever it is they are planning. In that moment, something hardens in her, the sentimental attachments to the life she used to know broken by the opening door. *I will do it*, she thinks. *I will throw myself out the window on the way back.*

Elsie readies her face, making it blank, intent on depriving Gabusch and Thorn of any expression, knowing her plan is to win. But when the door opens, Gabusch and Thorn aren't there. Instead, her father and Direktor Hof stand beside the desk. Direktor Hof looks tense, the grim lines around his mouth undisguised by his reddish moustache and beard. Her father has aged, the gauntness of his face and stoop of his shoulders making him almost unrecognizable. Her father stares at her, nothing in his face. He looks past her, searching for someone else. Elsie realizes two things at once: Her father has come for her. Her father does not know her.

May 2013
Gabriola Island, Canada

MY FATHER SEES US, RAISES AN ARM. He kisses our cheeks, takes my bag and puts it in the back of the Ford beside a bag of groceries and adds the pieces of the stroller. The ferry traffic is pressed into the small parking lot beside the dock, the ferry white in the spring sun against the ocean and the arbutus trees that line the cove. I bundle Tatianna into the carseat in the back and jump in the passenger side.

"How is it?" I ask.

My father laughs and rolls his eyes. "They're selling crème fraîche at the supermarket."

This makes me laugh, too, though there is something in this laugh that is a little hard at the edges. The fifty-dollars down, fifty-dollars a-month parcels that were a siren call to young people in the early seventies are long gone. Waterfront lots cost half a million and the population is now the third oldest in the province.

"What time does she land?"

"Later this aft, four o'clock seaplane," he says. I think of my mother flying west, having settled my grandmother in the nursing home. On Skype, she looks large-eyed and slim-boned, like a child.

My father edges the Ford out of the lot, making the turn up the ferry hill. I check on Tatianna in the back and see her face patterned with the shadows of the passing trees. As I look, I realize how long it has been since the children of the beach reached for the highest of the golden plums. The wide-armed circlers in their patchouli-scented skirts have largely moved on, to Lasqueti or Saturna or farther north, seeking the last of that kind of life.

When we reach the house, still framed by Douglas fir, we unload our luggage and the groceries. My father takes Tatianna down to the garden to examine the kale patch and swat at the apple blossoms. In the kitchen, everything is where it should be: onions in the wooden cabinet, oregano in the spice rack, canned tomatoes in the pantry. I wash my hands in the metallic glint of the sink. The sun shines through the skylights and the stained glass, creating coloured patterns on the oak floors.

I find the recipe I am looking for in the black binder on the shelf under the kitchen counter, handwritten in English with a strong Slavic slant. I put on a pot of rice, cut through the cabbage on the wide wooden board, and shuck the leaves from the core. I boil the cabbage leaves, drain them in a colander and use half a dozen of the leaves to create a protective layer at the bottom of a 10" x 14" aluminum baking pan. In the meantime, I make a tomato sauce in one pan, frying onion and garlic, adding canned tomatoes, seasoning salt, brown sugar, and oregano. In another, I fry a cup of ground beef and drain it. I then combine half the sauce with the rice and meat and keep the rest aside. When everything is ready, I spread out the ingredients on the counter, taking my time, wanting to get it right.

I take a cabbage leaf, place two tablespoons of rice mixture at the end of the leaf closest to me, roll it on the wooden board, fold in the ends, roll, keeping tension in the leaf, then squeeze the completed package in my palm. I spread tomato sauce across the the leaves in the baking pan and place the roll on the sauce. I pick up another leaf, start again, and think about Elsie Kühn-Leitz.

After my grandmother's departure from the house, Elsie continued to live at Haus Friedwart with her father and children. Elsie and Kurt Kühn divorced in 1948. Postwar, the house became a cultural hub for musicians, photographers, and politicians, an extension of her founding of the Wetzlar cultural society and her efforts in Franco-German rapprochement. Later, she championed Albert Schweitzer's hospital in Gabon and advocated for Congolese independence. Elsie Kühn-Leitz died in Wetzlar at the age of eighty-one. There is a street named after her in Avignon and another in Wetzlar, a street that can be seen from the house.

What I wonder about, still, is who Elsie Kühn-Leitz was writing for in 1947. As a lawyer, she understood the value of testimony, though the essay is rarely referenced. It is unlikely she could have imagined the directions this piece of writing might travel, least of all into the hands of the granddaughter of the woman who once bought her groceries. But fate is funny, which is reassuring. It suggests there is an unpredictable element. The possibility, at least, of alterations to the pattern.

As I mull all of this, the pan fills: four rolls across, six down. I add another layer of tomato sauce, cover the pan in aluminum foil, and put it in the oven at 350°F.

My father brings Tatianna up from the garden, her hands and face covered in mud. I wash her face and fingers as my father drives off to collect my mother from the seaplane dock. The seaplane streaks west into the sun, bringing my mother home, bearing her home over the ocean, the gulf between city and island, bringing with her the lace tablecloth and the last of my grandmother's story.

April 1946
Wetzlar, Germany

WHEN SERGEI RETURNS TO THE HOSPITAL in the Polish camp, he brings
two things with him: a baby stroller and a set of forged documents,
both purchased with the money from Frau Elsie. Irina's place of
birth is now listed as Tarnapol and Sergei's as Lemberg, two Polish
towns outside of Soviet control. The forger tells Sergei to forget
their last name. He gives them a new one, improbably long but pass-
ably authentic.

With the last of Frau Elsie's reichsmarks, Irina and Sergei buy
train tickets from Wetzlar to Wiesbaden, to the DP camp they hope
will be their last on the way to somewhere new. As the train pulls out
of the station, Irina looks back on Wetzlar. The church is badly dam-
aged, burnt out in parts, bombed in the last days of the war. There had
been the terrible noise of it, the sick dread on Frau Elsie's face as the
bombs started to fall, the panic in the house. But there had also been
the sorrow of the next morning when Irina, Friedrich, and Frau Elsie

had driven into town, stained glass shards and organ keys scattered across the road.

As they leave the American zone, Irina feels Sergei tense beside her. At the end of the train car, two Russian soldiers have appeared through the doors, checking papers. Sergei pulls the forged documents from the inside pocket of his brown suit, feigning boredom. Irina holds Alex tightly. The taller of the two Russians flicks his eyes over their papers, examines Irina and Sergei in their good clothes, hands back the papers, moves on. Irina breathes through her nose, and presses the back of her suit, wet with sweat, into the rough fabric of the train seat.

Two rows ahead, Irina hears the raised voice of one of the soldiers — "Documenti, sichas!" — followed by the pleading protests of a young couple with a dark-haired toddler.

The soldiers roust the family out of their seats and push them roughly down the aisle. The toddler clings to her mother's chest, her dark eyes enormous.

June 2013
Vancouver and Niagara Falls

SUMMER COMES AND EVERYTHING LOOKS DIFFERENT. John and I take Tatianna down to English Bay, one of her hands in each of ours as she toddles along the path. We join the crowd of pleasure seekers, laughing and forgetful.

The next day, Tatianna and I fly east to join my mother and grandmother in Alliston. As the taxi driver lets us out in the nursing home parking lot, I take in the garden, the gazebo, the low-rise, flat-topped central building. Beside the gazebo, there is a pond with a stone statue of a frog. I push the stroller down the cement path and through the sliding doors. Inside the nursing home, it smells like disinfectant and floor polish, generic institutional, and I relax, slightly. Tatianna and I walk through the main foyer into a narrower hallway on the left as instructed by my mother, past a series of small, brightly lit rooms and find my grandmother's at the end of the corridor. The card outside the door says Irene Nikifortchuk. Inside, I can hear my mother's voice and lower, quieter responses from my grandmother. I knock and we roll in. My grandmother lies on a single bed, family pictures on the blue walls around her.

There are hugs and greetings. I park the stroller in a corner between a blue armchair and my grandmother's wheelchair. Tatianna plays with my grandmother's fingers and the sheet where it hangs off the bed. I study my grandmother. Whatever pain she is in, the anxiety she has always carried in the lines around her mouth has receded and her skin looks smooth and firm. Her hair is thick and whiter, framing her strong features.

"She looks good," I say to my mother as my grandmother and Tatianna play.

"She does," my mother says quietly. "But her memory is failing. She has a hard time remembering breakfast, though she can still talk about fifty years ago. She keeps slipping into the past."

My grandmother's eyes drift away from Tatianna and out the window into the garden. She blinks as my mother and I near the bed.

"How are you feeling, Mom?" my mother asks.

"Hungry," my grandmother says.

"Well, that's okay. It's dinner time. Why don't you go down to the dining room for something? You don't have to get dressed for dinner, here, no one does."

My grandmother looks askance.

"If people naked, I not going."

"No, Mom," my mother says, reassuring her. "I mean people don't get dressed up for dinner. You can just wear the jogging suit you have on."

"Oh," my grandmother says, chuckling. "Okay. I go then."

We walk my grandmother down to the dining room, where a chalkboard with fancy script lists the choice of baked trout or ravioli. There is a salad course to start and apple crumble for dessert. Five or six elderly people sit at each of the six tables, which are covered in checked tablecloths. The residents stare at Tatianna and there is hunger there, too, in the way the very old look at the very young.

An elderly man in a grey cardigan pats Tatianna's arm. "Stay young, baby," he says. "Stay young."

My mother, Tatianna, and I step out to the garden while my grand-mother eats. Tatianna plays with the stone frog. In the last few months, her arms have become supple and elongated, her belly flattening into a more defined torso.

When we return to my grandmother's room after the dinner hour, she is sitting in her blue armchair, one hand clasped tightly in the other. "Lucy," my grandmother says when she sees us. "I so hungry. The guards no feed us here. So much food in Germany and they give us nothing, only enough to keep working."

The blood drains out of my mother's face and I feel slapped. Tatianna frets, pulls at the neckline of my blouse. A machine beeps faintly in the room next door.

My mother's eyes travel around the room searching for some kind of answer. There is no answer, but she focuses in on the wheelchair against the wall.

"Okay, Mom," she says, her voice steady. "Let's get out of here. You want to go for a ride?"

My grandmother is still for a moment, then nods. We help her into the wheelchair. I buckle Tatianna into the stroller and we are off, down the hallway, heading toward the shops of central Alliston. The escape is temporary but there it was.

"Ice cream, Mom?" my mother asks.

"Yes," my grandmother says. "Butterscotch. Big one."

Tatianna picks up on the word ice cream and brightens. From some distant reservoir, she begins to sing the song I sang when she was very small, in a strong voice, strangely deep and atonal, "We're going for a ride in a char-iot, char-iot, char-iot —"

We exit through the sliding glass doors. Around us, the evening is still, the tops of the trees barely moving, their branches full of yellow light. It is one of those evenings we rarely have on the coast, where the humidity settles into something deep and warm and languorous.

AFTERWORD

MY GRANDMOTHER WAS BORN ON Elsie Kühn-Leitz's nineteenth birthday in 1922. She died ninety-two years later on May 11, 2014, my thirty-sixth birthday, eleven months after this visit. One hundred kilometres north of the nursing home in Alliston, Leica built a factory in Midland in the early 1950s. While the Midland plant was smaller than the factory in Wetzlar, the blueprints for the interior workspaces are largely identical.

ACKNOWLEDGEMENTS

THE RESEARCH FOR THIS BOOK WAS made possible by the Social Sciences and Humanities Research Council of Canada (with thanks to Bev Neufeld) and the thoughtful research inquiries and translation work of Kerstin Stuerzbecher. I am grateful to my editor, Susan Renouf, for finding the book in the draft and for deftly helping me see it through. I would like to thank Baharak Yousefi at the SFU Library and the staff at the Ukrainian Canadian Research & Documentation Centre in Toronto as well as Susanne Eichhorn at the German Consulate General Vancouver. In Germany, the project was helped along by the Wetzlar Historical Society, particularly by Bernd Lindenthal as well as by Petra Hannig of the City of Wetzlar Historical Archives with thanks to Wolfgang Wiedl. The manuscript was made more accurate and detailed by the careful reading and suggestions of Dr. Oliver Nass, Cornelia's son and Elsie Kühn-Leitz's grandson. I owe him a significant debt for this as well as for his moving and generous correspondence.

I learned a great deal at the 2016 German Studies Association Conference in San Diego and the 2018 Beyond Camps and Forced Labour conference organized by Birkbeck, University of London, the Wiener Library, and the Imperial War Museums, with thanks to The Foundation Remembrance, Responsibility, and Future for funding my participation. Students, alumni, faculty (particularly Stephen Duguid), staff, and Shadbolt Fellow, Yosef Wosk, of SFU's Graduate Liberal Studies Program, created a supportive culture of ideas in which I did much of my thinking about this book. Suzanne Bardgett, David Chariandy, Theresa Kishkan, Richard Mackie, Susan Mertens, Simona Mitroiu, Catriona Strang, Alan Twigg and Max Wyman provided encouragement and publishing suggestions that led to this project finding a home with ECW. In turn, the staff at ECW were expert and enthusiastic in all aspects of the book's production. Photographs were provided by the City of Wetzlar — Historical Archives, Alex Nikifortchuk, the Ernst Leitz Foundation and the Archive Ralf Schnitzler (the last two courtesy of Oliver Nass) with my thanks.

This book is about my family, for my family, and could not have been written without their love and support.

This book is also available as a Global Certified Accessible™ (GCA) ebook. ECW Press's ebooks are screen reader friendly and are built to meet the needs of those who are unable to read standard print due to blindness, low vision, dyslexia, or a physical disability.

At ECW Press, we want you to enjoy our books in whatever format you like. If you've bought a print copy just send an email to ebook@ecwpress.com and include:

- the book title
- the name of the store where you purchased it
- a screenshot or picture of your order/receipt number and your name
- your preference of file type: PDF (for desktop reading), ePub (for a phone/tablet, Kobo, or Nook), mobi (for Kindle)

A real person will respond to your email with your ebook attached. Please note this offer is only for copies bought for personal use and does not apply to school or library copies.

Thank you for supporting an independently owned Canadian publisher with your purchase!